THE TRUE STORY
OF THE CHRISTMAS TRUCE

THE TRUE STORY OF THE CHRISTMAS TRUCE

British and German Eyewitness Accounts from the First World War

Anthony Richards

Foreword by Hew Strachan
Translations by Eva Burke

For Lisette & Michael with a thank you from "Kingswood" surrounded by the designs you created for us. In gratitude.

Greenhill Books

for Malcolm

*The True Story of the Christmas Truce:
British and German Eyewitness Accounts from the First World War*

Greenhill Books

First published by Greenhill Books, 2021
Greenhill Books, c/o Pen & Sword Books Ltd,
47 Church Street, Barnsley, S. Yorkshire, S70 2AS
For more information on our books, please visit
www.greenhillbooks.com, email contact@greenhillbooks.com
or write to us at the above address.

Copyright © Anthony Richards, 2021

All rights reserved. No part of this publication may be reproduced, stored in or introduced into a retrieval system, or transmitted, in any form, or by any means (electronic, mechanical, photocopying, recording or otherwise) without the prior written permission of the publisher. Any person who does any unauthorised act in relation to this publication may be liable to criminal prosecution and civil claims for damages.

CIP data records for this title are available from the British Library
ISBN 978-1-78438-614-6

Typeset by JCS Publishing Services Ltd
Typeset in 12/15pt Palatino Linotype
Printed and bound by CPI Group (UK) Ltd, Croydon, CR0 4YY

Contents

List of Illustrations	vii
Foreword by Hew Strachan	ix
Introduction	1
1 Digging In	9
2 Christmas Approaches	34
3 Christmas Eve in the British Sector	58
4 Christmas Day in the British Sector	77
5 The Christmas Truce Elsewhere	118
6 Boxing Day and Afterwards	139
7 Causes	162
8 Legacy	181
Conclusion	204
Acknowledgements	208
Notes	209
Select Bibliography and Sources	222
Index	224

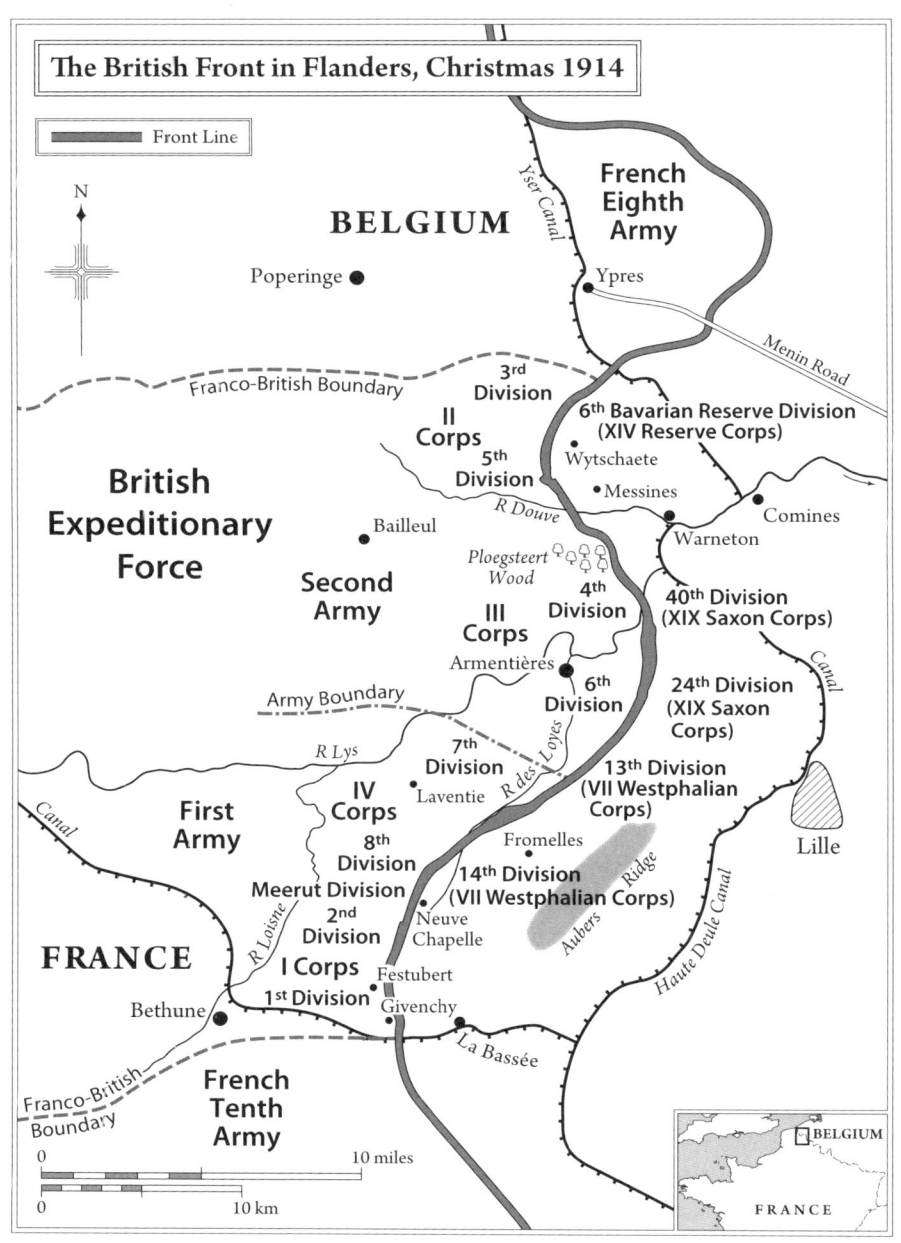

Christmas Truce 1914

Illustrations

1. Pope Benedict XV (1854–1922)
2. Field Marshal Sir John French (1852–1925), commander of the British Expeditionary Force.
3. General Sir Horace Smith-Dorrien (1858–1930), commander of the British II Corps and, from 26 December 1914, Second Army.
4. General Sir Douglas Haig (1861–1928), commander of the British I Corps and, from 26 December 1914, First Army.
5. Rupprecht, Crown Prince of Bavaria (1869–1955), commander of the German Sixth Army.
6. German soldiers singing carols in their trench, alongside a lit Christmas tree.
7. A typical German Christmas card from 1914.
8. This British Christmas card from 1914 stresses the partnership of the Allied nations.
9. Soldiers at the front would use whatever means they could to get a message home to their loved ones. This soldier chose to send home an annotated luggage label as a novel souvenir.
10. Around 400,000 gift boxes such as this were distributed to the British troops at Christmas 1914 on behalf of Princess Mary.
11. *The Illustrated London News* of 9 January 1915.
12. An internal illustration from the same journal gives an artist's depiction of the fraternisation.
13. Press coverage of the truce featured many photographs taken at the front by the participants.
14. *The Daily Mirror* of 8 January 1915.

15. Many commemorative coins were struck to mark the First World War centenary in 2014, including this Christmas Truce example. It is unfortunately based upon an original photograph incorrectly attributed to the infamous football match!
16. This modern memorial to the truce, 'All Together Now' by Andy Edwards, is located in the grounds of St Luke's Church, Liverpool.

Foreword

In 1914 the public appetite for news could not be fully eased by the printed press, despite its volume in terms of titles, print-runs and updated editions. Moreover, the imposition of censorship meant that readers were aware that that there were stories that were not being published. Rumours came to supplement – or sometimes replace – facts, as neighbours met on street corners and colleagues crossed paths when buying their morning papers or consulting the ticker tapes in their clubs and offices. Gossip generated myths and legends. Some had religious connotations and others predictive power. It was said that British soldiers at Mons had seen angels disguised as archers who had protected them from the Germans on the night of 23 August 1914. Later in the war, some came to believe, as they passed through Albert on their way up to the Somme front, that the war would end when the vertiginously leaning Virgin fell from the spire of the town's church. An early example of such myths was the expectation in 1914 that the war would be over by Christmas. Devoid of clear authorship or strategic rationalisation, it reflected the potency and convening power of Christian Europe's festive conclusion to each year. It revived the hopes of bewildered and discombobulated peoples by giving immediate comfort and promising a return to normality in the near future.

The stories of the Christmas Truce of 1914 can seem to belong in this fantasy world. They testified to the essential decency of mankind, to a sense of common humanity in the midst of war, and even to divine intervention. They suggested that Christ on earth could not tolerate the killing on his birthday. Through their embellishment, they have become part of the warp and woof of contemporary popular understanding of the First World War, today sanctified less by the faith of churchgoers than by the surrogate religion of football. In 2014 the reports that erstwhile enemies had played a friendly match in No Man's Land were incorporated into the war's centenary commemorations. So, one hundred years on, the Christmas Truce fed another fantasy: the suggestion that sport can replace war in the sublimation of national rivalries. In the process the Christmas Truce trivialised the seriousness of the endeavours in which the players of 1914 were actually engaged.

Conveniently the current telling of the legend also ignores military common sense. Armies in France and Flanders were inherently unlikely to fight on Christmas Day. In mid-winter the days in north-western Europe were too short for sustained operations and the weather too unpredictable to permit their planning. December was a quiet month. In a way that mobile operations had not, the static nature of trench warfare and the proximity of the front lines provided the opportunity for communication across No Man's Land. Furthermore, truces could have practical utility. They provided an opportunity to bury the dead. They enabled keen-eyed officers to cross No Man's Land unimpeded, so as to check the identity of the enemy units they faced and to assess the strengths and weaknesses of their positions. Later in the war, in 1917, following the revolution in Petrograd and the abdication of the Tsar, the German Army on the Eastern Front used the Orthodox celebration of Easter to fraternise with Russian soldiers, with the specific intention of further undermining their will to fight. Similarly, for some Russians it was a chance to spread the values of international socialism in

FOREWORD

the enemy's ranks. In 1918 truces at Easter were used in comparable ways on the Italian front. A truce could be used as a weapon of war.

British and German generals on the Western Front knew that and so sought to suppress the reports that Christmas 1914 had been marked by truces on the front line and disciplined those officers who had permitted them to occur. Their efforts backfired. Rumour and gossip elevated and inflated the story. Even if most of the Western Front was comparatively quiet on the morning of Christmas Day 1914, there was not a universal truce. Rather there was a series of independently negotiated and sometimes spontaneous acts of fraternisation which acquired a cumulative significance in hindsight that they lacked at the time. The contacts were localised. They seem barely to have touched the French Army, which held the bulk of the line on the Western Front. It confronted an enemy who now occupied a significant chunk of its homeland and held many of its people in his hands. These were not conditions conducive to manifestations of the Christian spirit. Perhaps, too, the anti-Catholicism of Protestant Germany made fraternisation less possible with the French than the British.

Nonetheless, the point remains: there really were truces on the Western Front on Christmas Day in 1914, and first rumour and then legend had a foundation in fact, not fantasy. Moreover, although local, contained and driven from the 'bottom up', there were enough of them for the phenomenon to be significant in its own right. Peace in war was – and is – possible, however paradoxical. A shared sense of humanity can, albeit fleetingly, cut across enmity. And such stories, however challenging to the tropes of military discipline, serve to reinforce a sense of optimism about the long run, however dire the immediate circumstances. Anthony Richards has written an account of the truces of Christmas 1914 which cuts through the myth by dint of careful and thorough scholarship, sustained over a long period and embracing sources from Germany as well as Britain. The result is not only revealing, it is also eminently readable.

Hew Strachan

Introduction

It'll all be over by Christmas.[1]

SUCH WAS THE WIDELY shared hope held by many families in August 1914, at the very beginning of the First World War. Some kind of European conflict had been far from unexpected, with the increased militarisation of Imperial Germany threatening the fragile balance of power between European nations. The network of political and military alliances that existed between countries, built up over many years, meant that once a conflict broke out it would irrevocably draw in multiple combatants, along with their empires, ensuring that any war would become a truly global phenomenon. Yet few expected a war to last for so long. In the minds of many observers from both sides, it felt natural to expect a relatively short, sharp conflict, centred in Europe, in order to resolve the territorial disputes rather than anything longer term. Few if any would have predicted that the war would continue for another four years.

When Christmas arrived in 1914, barely four months after the outbreak of war, it proved to be an important moment for each nation to pause and process how the circumstances were affecting individual lives. As with any Christmas holiday, it was a time when everybody wanted to let off steam, to forget the difficulties they had been experiencing in everyday life and concentrate instead upon the need for selfish indulgence. The approach of the year's end was also the traditional time for reflection on the previous twelve months, leading people to consider their priorities and hopes for the future. Yet this particular year's Christmas celebrations would be affected by one very significant factor: the major European nations were fighting a brutal war. How could people really celebrate the season of goodwill during a time of hateful, bloody conflict? Christmas would no longer be the peaceful holiday that everybody expected, since world events had overtaken any individual concerns. But it gave people from both sides an opportunity to reflect on the reasons why they were fighting, and the likelihood of the war being resolved in the immediate future.

Some, including those not yet quite convinced of the likely prospect of an extended conflict, looked to Christmas as an excuse for accelerating peace. The First World War would see an unprecedented level of civilian debate which can be observed quite clearly in the newspapers and magazines of 1914 and remains crucial for understanding how people felt about the conflict at the end of that year. The expansion of war reportage brought the fighting directly into the living rooms of those back home, where people would debate the course of the war, offer praise to military heroes of the hour and circulate stories (often of dubious reliability) concerning enemy atrocities and their opponents' overall 'beastliness'. Everybody had an opinion and the all-encompassing nature of the war meant that there was an eager audience ready to listen. Thus by the end of the year a number of initiatives for peace had already appeared which, although ultimately unsuccessful, meant that the idea of a Christmas armistice was certainly in people's minds as a possibility, albeit remote.

One of the most important factors which made that first Christmas of the war so different from Christmases of previous wars was the great number of men serving overseas. Earlier conflicts had largely been fought by professional armies, highly regimented and trained to obey orders, trusting in their military hierarchy to make the right winning decisions. But the need to expand the initial peacetime British Expeditionary Force (BEF) of 70,000 men to cope with the greater scale of the challenge on the Western Front meant that for the first time a significant number of soldiers serving overseas were from the Territorial Force: keen volunteers, known as 'weekend soldiers', who most likely had never suspected that they might be called to carry arms against an enemy in a foreign country.

Many families would therefore come together to share their Christmas dinner in 1914 with an empty place at their table for the first time; from Britain alone, by the end of the year some 270,000 men were serving overseas as part of the BEF while thousands more were already in the enemy's hands as prisoners of war. In addition, almost 27,500 had made the ultimate sacrifice on behalf of their country and would never be returning home.[2] This sense of separation – either temporary or permanent – would have been palpable in the last few months of 1914, and Christmas only made it worse. Those on the home fronts of both Britain and Germany would soon realise that the war was going to run and run, with no obvious end in sight.

Separation from loved ones back home would have been particularly felt by the soldiers in the field, to whom it would also have been apparent by Christmas that the war had reached a turning point. The initial war of movement had by now settled into a deadlock, with both sides digging in to prepare for the winter. Christmas 1914 saw the front-line soldiers fully entrenched in these defensive positions, maintaining a stalemate which would last until at least the following spring. Over the previous month or two there had been a gradual realisation that trench fighting would form the basic strategy for the rest of the conflict, and by Christmas both those in the field and the public back home had come to accept the necessity of this unexpected form of siege warfare.

Traditionally a time for reflection when people would also look forward to the future, Christmas meant that hopes and fears were at an all-time high as the end of the year approached. It is perhaps fitting that this important first Christmas of the war would become even more memorable by the unique event which was about to happen on the Western Front, particularly between the strip of front-line trenches running through an area of Flanders, with the town of Ypres to the north and La Bassée to the south.

Every British infantry battalion on active service kept a daily war diary, usually written by the unit's subaltern, recounting the incidents of note in which they were involved. The official record kept by the 1st Battalion, Somerset Light Infantry, contains the following entry for Christmas Day, 25 December 1914, when it was based in the 4th Division front-line trenches of the St Yves sector.

> There was much singing in the trenches last night by both sides. Germans opposite us brought up their regimental band and played theirs and our national anthems followed by 'Home, Sweet Home'. A truce was mutually arranged by the men in the trenches. During the morning officers met the German officers halfway between the trenches and it was arranged that we should bring in our dead who were lying between the trenches. The bodies of Captain Maud, Captain Orr and 2nd Lieutenant Henson were brought in, also those of 18 NCOs and men. They were buried the same day. The Germans informed us that they had captured a wounded officer and this was thought to be 2nd Lieutenant K. G. G. Dennys who commanded one of the attacking platoons of B Company on the 19th. There was a sharp frost last night which continued during the day, and the weather

INTRODUCTION

was very seasonable. Not a shot or shell was fired by either side in our neighbourhood; and both sides walked about outside their trenches quite unconcernedly. It afforded a good opportunity for inspecting our trenches by daylight. The enemy's works were noticed to be very strong. A very peaceful day.[3]

Incredibly, this was no one-off incident. This single unit's fraternisation with their enemy mirrored the experience shared by many others in Flanders which, collectively, led to a large-scale ceasefire which would become known as the Christmas Truce. British and German soldiers chatted together, local armistices were hastily arranged and direct fraternisation occurred out in No Man's Land, the neutral area between the front-line trenches. Food was swapped, jokes shared and games of football enjoyed. Such arrangements varied according to different sectors, but the truce largely began on Christmas Eve and often incorporated Christmas Day and Boxing Day at the very least; some sectors were still enjoying peaceful agreements in the first few days of the New Year. But the arrangements rarely lasted for much longer than this. It was a relatively short-term event, conducted on an informal basis by those in the front line, and was quickly brought to a halt by the senior commanders of both sides once the seriousness and scale of the truce became more widely known.

The Christmas Truce would come to be seen in later years as something of a blip in the regular conduct of the war, almost an embarrassment which military commentators from both sides were keen to portray as an anomaly. It conflicted with the patriotic nationalism which was expected to be demonstrated by both sides, since their respective armies were fighting to win a war, not make friends with one another. It also served to highlight in a rather perfect way the great dichotomy existing between war and faith. How can you fight a war of aggression while also celebrating Christmas, the traditional time for peace and goodwill? For those reasons the Christmas Truce was increasingly regarded as unimportant to the larger narrative and awkward to fit into the standard account. Even during the First World War itself, some came to doubt whether the event had ever really happened in the first place, and it began to enter into the realm of wartime myths, in a similar way to the 'Angels of Mons'.

But the Christmas Truce *did* happen and there remains a wealth of historical evidence to corroborate the event. Some mysteries about it do remain, most notably the truth behind the now-legendary game of football which was alleged to have been played between teams of British and German soldiers, but there is no doubt at all that the widespread fraternisation and temporary armistice of Christmas certainly occurred.

The events on the Western Front over Christmas 1914 continue to raise a number of important and interesting questions. How was it possible for such a widespread truce to happen in the first place, especially considering the harsh fighting which had been going on between the very same soldiers only days before? Perhaps even more puzzling is the fact that the armistice did not carry on indefinitely; once it was considered to be over, both sides would largely resume their normal warlike mentality very quickly indeed and in many cases were happily firing at the same enemy with whom they had been sharing meals and handshakes mere hours before. Some have attempted to portray the Christmas Truce as a kind of proletarian uprising, with working men deliberately dropping their rifles in order to embrace their fellow man in a sort of socialist brotherhood. But little or no historical testimony appears to exist from

INTRODUCTION

any participants to reinforce this notion, the simple fact of the matter being that the fraternisation was a spontaneous occurrence without any bigger, longer-lasting plan.

Much of the historiography on the subject of the Christmas Truce tends to concentrate on the events leading up to the ceasefire and why the soldiers decided to put down their arms for that brief period. The reasons why the front-line troops chose to fraternise are in many ways quiet straightforward and self-evident, yet the real question should perhaps centre on why the decision was made to resume fighting afterwards. We will also look at the aftermath of the Christmas Truce. Why did an event of similar scale fail to occur again, either in that war or any subsequent one?

The definitive book on the Christmas Truce has been that written by Malcolm Brown and Shirley Seaton, originally published in 1984 and subsequently reissued in various updated editions, most notably for the event's eightieth anniversary in 1994. I knew Malcolm very well indeed since he was a regular visitor to my office in the Imperial War Museum over many years, and while I would regularly point him towards new archival sources for his various First World War books he would in turn regale me and my fellow archivists with entertaining stories of the many war veterans he had met and interviewed. He had a genuine affection for those men who directly experienced the Christmas Truce and I share in that desire to see their first-hand testimony circulated as widely as possible. Now that none of the original combatants from the First World War is still alive, we of course rely more than ever on those invaluable written and recorded experiences.

For these reasons, the main encouragement for me to write this book lay in the fresh availability of a wealth of rarely seen German accounts of the Christmas Truce, many never before translated into English and some not previously published. The story of the truce has traditionally been a very British-centric one, but for the first time we can begin to look more at the event as a shared experience between two opposing sides who decided, just for a brief moment, to put aside their differences and celebrate the true meaning of Christmas.

CHAPTER ONE

Digging In

To BEST COMPREHEND THE events that would transpire on the Western Front towards the end of December 1914, we should appreciate the situation in which the participants found themselves during that year's final few months. Trench warfare determined the conditions under which the soldiers of both sides fought and lived, and this experience would inevitably influence their behaviour towards accepting the possibility of a ceasefire at Christmas time.

While the assassination of the Austro-Hungarian heir to the throne on 28 June 1914 by a Serbian gunman is often highlighted as the spark which ignited Europe into a major conflict, it would be much more accurate to point to the intertwined military and political alliances between countries which existed at that time. These served to ensure that one nation after the next was pulled into what became known as the First World War. An Austro-Hungarian declaration of war against Serbia on 28 July led to mass mobilisation of armies across Europe. The military and naval rivalries which had existed between nations for so many decades were now given the opportunity to be fully expressed. Germany declared war on France on 3 August, marching into neutral Belgium the following day and pushing Britain to declare war against the invader. To begin with, Germany and Austria-Hungary would face a war on two European fronts, with Russia holding them back in the east and the alliance of Britain, France and Belgium facing them in the west. More and more nations came to be involved as the British Empire rallied its considerable colonial forces, with Indian troops arriving on the Western

Front by the end of the year, and soldiers from Australia, New Zealand, Canada and South Africa preparing to enter the conflict.

A relatively small British Expeditionary Force of some 90,000 men, under the overall command of Field Marshal Sir John French, began to embark for France on 15 August. The first few months of the conflict were characterised by fairly mobile warfare, a remarkably different form of fighting from that which would become the norm for the next four years. Few could have predicted how the conflict would develop, with naive patriotic enthusiasm for a quick clash forming the common mood in both Britain and Germany. F. L. Cassel, a reservist in the German infantry, recalled that initial feeling:

> We had no idea what horrors, what suffering was ahead of us. There was *Enthusiasmus* and conviction of victory, in spite of the fact that we had no vision of war, of the adversaries, their weapons. Nobody had heard grenades burst or bullets whistle. There were no casualty lists.[1]

The First World War began as a quick-moving conflict, the German Army sweeping through Belgium to be halted only momentarily by a number of short confrontations with the French, Belgians and British. The initial decisive moment was the Battle of Mons on 23 August, the first battle of the war in which the British were properly involved, followed swiftly by another short but ferocious clash at Le Cateau three days later. These two German victories, one after the other, led to a mass retreat of the Allies back towards Paris. The German Army's advance was only halted by the French stand at the Battle of the Marne, beginning on 6 September, and the follow-up clash on the Aisne a week later saw both sides digging in and forming entrenched positions of defence. The only way forward for either side was now to outflank one another, and there therefore followed the so-called 'Race to the Sea' in which the Franco-British and German armies rushed northwards in a series of attempts to outflank each other through Picardy, Artois and Flanders, constantly advancing towards the Belgian coast. Neither side was able to gain any major advantage. Instead, by 19 October both armies ended up largely entrenched, with the front line running from Nieuport on the Belgian coast right down to the French border with Switzerland to the south.

While trenches had been dug in earlier conflicts, most recently the South African wars at the turn of the century, they had usually been regarded as short-term solutions. The more siege-like situation of the First World War and the immense scale of entrenchment which this involved, as well as the corresponding necessity to adapt tactics and weaponry, were new concepts for both sides to take in. This was certainly recognised by Major H. D. W. Lloyd of the 2nd Battalion, The Cameronians:

> The accounts of the present fighting all show that we have had to alter our tactics, and that modern artillery has not only got ahead of fortresses, but also of infantry. As a result, everyone is digging, a process the British infantry man is not too fond of. Even shell fire, unless heavy, does not overcome his distaste. But from what I can gather, we have got to dig our way into Germany.[2]

Stalemate was also the case on the Eastern Front. A major clash near Tannenberg between Russia and Germany had been fought at the very end of August, giving an important German victory. The Russian Second Army was almost completely destroyed as a result, and a series of subsequent battles also shattered much of their First Army. The Russians would effectively be kept out of action until spring of the following year, although the German need to garrison the Western Front meant that the invader remained outnumbered and on the defensive in the east.

As well as defending their own territory, there was a clear diplomatic need on the part of the Western Allies to assist their Russian friends by keeping up pressure on the Germans in the west. One final attempt to influence the stalemate on the Western Front in 1914 concentrated on the sector surrounding the Belgian town of Ypres, which remained the vital route for any northerly German invasion. The First Battle of Ypres lasted until 22 November and saw the town liberated from a brief German occupation, with the BEF establishing itself in and around the surrounding salient in order to protect this key strategic location.

The first mobile phase of the war was now over. The Germans decided to switch to a defensive stance on the Western Front to allow them to move troops east to reinforce against the Russians, and they began to dig in for the winter. Although the British, French and Belgians were more inclined to continue with their attempts to push the Germans back, they were rather limited in terms of options. Trench warfare was heavily reliant upon the weather, and as winter approached, the deteriorating conditions thus proved increasingly unconducive to any offensive action. The Allies therefore followed suit and dug in; entrenchment would be the name of the game from now on.

Winter was, generally speaking, the worst time for a soldier living and fighting in a trench. Spending so much time in holes in the ground meant that their well-being was directly linked to the climate, as Henry Williamson, later to become famous as an author of popular books such as *Tarka the Otter*, would recall as a lowly rifleman:

One night in the second week of November [1914] there was a tremendous storm blowing, lightning was flashing and flares were still going up. Rain splashed up about nine or ten inches in No Man's Land, and it went on and on and on. That stopped the First Battle of Ypres which was raging up north. Our sector north of Armentières ceased. The condition of the latrines can be imagined and we could not sleep, every minute was like an hour. The dead were lying out in front. The rains kept on, we were in yellow clay, and the water table was 2 feet below. Our trenches were 7-foot deep. We walked about or moved very slowly in marl or pug of yellow watery clay. When the evening came and we could get out of it, it took about an hour to climb out. Some of our chaps slipped in and were drowned. They couldn't even be seen, but were trodden on later. We were relieved after the fourth night and some of us had to be carried out. I noticed that many of the tough ones were carried out, while the skinny little whippersnappers like myself could somehow manage, we got out somehow as we had not the weight to carry. We marched back – slouched back – and eventually got to our billet at Ploegsteert, a mile and a half away. We fell on the floor and slept, equipment on and everything. Everything was mud-slapped – overcoats, boots and everything. We were dead beat.[3]

Trench warfare was initially considered to be a temporary, albeit necessary, evil. Neither side seriously planned to be in the same situation come the spring, since the common hope was that offensive actions would succeed in breaking the deadlock. However, there was a growing recognition within the respective High Commands that their armies were effectively experiencing a form of siege warfare. The only factors that would make a difference to the status quo would be a massive influx of troops, weaponry and ammunition to benefit one side, or for one nation's army to become so weakened that the balance of power might shift against them.

Until either of those possibilities could occur, the war on the Western Front therefore developed into a series of continual small-scale attacks undertaken by each side. These were often little more than trench raids or skirmishes, resulting in small but regular numbers of casualties and little significant territorial gain. There would still be intermittent fighting on a much larger scale, characterised by carefully planned battles which were designed to act as the next 'big push' to make a difference. Yet rarely did these find success in the way they intended, until towards the end of the war when conditions began to change in the Allies' favour.

Despite being forced to engage in trench warfare towards the end of 1914, the French and Belgians felt reluctant to do so. This was completely understandable, considering that they were defending their home territory and were therefore keener to keep up the offensive action to take advantage of any shift of German troops eastwards to Russia. The British too were not overly keen to dig in completely, since they were particularly concerned by the German occupation of Antwerp and the Belgian coast, which presented an equally important territorial threat by allowing Germany's fleet to challenge the Royal Navy's dominance of the North Sea. While this threat was for the moment a largely speculative one, its seriousness would be proven as the war progressed. Germany's U-boats and its surface fleet would operate out of Antwerp, Ostend and Zeebrugge and threaten the supply of food not only to the armies in France, but to the mouths of those in the Britain Isles themselves.

This shared reluctance to completely embrace trench warfare was characterised by the decision to launch one final offensive before the winter set in, and as the dominant partner among the Allies at this time, France would largely call the shots. General Joseph Joffre therefore ordered a series of attacks to begin on 14 December before the wintry conditions made any further campaigning too difficult. As these attacks coincided with the troops' preparations for their first Christmas in the trenches, and would have a direct connection to the Christmas Truce, we will look at these operations in greater detail in the following chapter.

*

By the end of December 1914, ten British infantry divisions and four cavalry divisions held a front line of about 30 miles in total, running from St Elois, just south of Ypres, to Givenchy next to the La Bassée canal. By this time there were almost 270,000 officers and men of the British and Indian armies based on the Western Front, under the overall command of Field Marshal Sir John French. French had distinguished himself as a cavalry officer during the campaign in the Sudan in 1884–85 as well as the Boer War at the turn of the century, and shortly before the First World War had been appointed Chief of the Imperial General Staff (CIGS). In this role, he had controversially insisted on the importance of cavalry training at a time when such tactics were increasingly seen as outdated. French was reputed to possess a somewhat abrasive personality and was by all accounts not an easy man to get along with.

The main German formation facing the British in Flanders was the Sixth Army, under Crown Prince Rupprecht of Bavaria. A younger man than French (he was 45 at the beginning of the war, while French was aged 61), Rupprecht was the eldest child of Ludwig III, the last king of Bavaria. Although his appointment as commander of the Sixth Army came automatically as a result of his status as a senior royal, he was an extremely conscientious officer and proved a more than capable commander. This was largely due to the extent of his pre-war military studies, as well as his professional attitude to leadership.

For those soldiers based in the Flanders trenches, any anticipation for a continued advance would have soon worn off to reveal a harsh and monotonous routine, characterised by poor living conditions associated with spending much of their time in the trenches and dugouts while under the constant threat of sudden death. The closeness of each side's trenches meant that in some areas the combatants were stationed as near as 30 yards from one another. Living in such close proximity, it was therefore inevitable that after a while the British, French and Belgian soldiers began to understand and empathise with their German opponents, and vice versa, leading to the widespread realisation that every soldier, regardless of his nationality, shared largely the same living conditions, regular duties and associated dangers, challenges and fears.

Relatively few soldiers would have had much experience of fighting a war, and their attitudes to the enemy would largely have been heavily influenced by propaganda and feelings towards their opponents displayed by people back home. Whichever nation a soldier was fighting for, his country's government propaganda sought to depict their respective enemy in overly hostile terms, encouraging aggression and justifying the necessity for war. Empathy caused by their proximity to the enemy meant that not all soldiers were so influenced in this way, with many simply feeling that they were there to 'get the job done', being ready and willing to fight their opponent yet without any personal grudges. Graham Williams, a rifleman who would come to be involved in the Christmas Day fraternisation, remembered how the attitude of the troops in the field was often noticeably different to that shown by those back home:

> Until we met [the Germans] we believed a lot of the stories in the papers and all the rest of it but we came to the conclusion after that they were just very much like ourselves. We didn't hate them at all. We were very much against the policy of the German government and the Kaiser particularly, but the individual Germans, well we thought they were just doing their job in the same way we were for their country. Although of course if there'd been an attack we would have shot them all right, the same as they'd have shot us. Being shot was a sort of occupational hazard and it applied to both sides and that's the way we sort of looked at it.
>
> I don't think I saw [a German] at all until the truce, that was about the first time. The first time I fired towards the enemy was the first time we went into the trenches. The London Rifle Brigade were attached as an extra battalion to 11th Infantry Brigade who were regulars ... and we went into the trenches first of all in small parties of about six at a time and we were put under the care of one of the regulars ... and he said, 'Well, there's the German parapet over there', so of course we immediately got up there and had a shot at it with our rifles, but I don't think there was anyone on the receiving end. The first time I shot at an actual German was during the Second Battle of Ypres [in May 1915, the following year].[4]

The relationship between ordinary soldiers and their senior commanders is also worth noting here. As with any hierarchical structure, the inclination of the lower workers is to blame the bosses, and there had already been a long tradition of this in both the British and German armies by the time that the First World War began. Such a sentiment was perhaps inevitable in a situation where individuals were being placed in regular danger as a result of decisions made by others. It was of course only worsened by the fact that the decision-makers were rarely seen and the logic of their orders may not have been immediately obvious to those in the trenches. Particular derision was aimed at the staff officers or 'red tabs', the generals and commanders of units much higher up the chain of command than the lowly infantry battalion.

Effectively, there was a noticeable reputational split between combatants and non-combatants, the latter of whom were rarely seen in the trenches and easily distinguishable from trench fighters. The perception that non-combatants enjoyed better overall living conditions and were rarely placed in situations of immediate danger led to bitterness from those in the front line. Interestingly, this attitude was not even particularly based on class differences or the clear distinction between officers and other ranks; rather, it was a simple recognition that life at the front and life behind the line were very different things. This attitude towards staff officers was shared by all nationalities; the opinion of Captain Gerald Burgoyne, serving with the Royal Irish Rifles in Flanders at the beginning of 1915, was very typical:

> The whole time I have been out here I never once saw any of our Brigade or Divisional Staff come up to the trenches, and the ground around is to all the staff a kind of *terra incognita*. I have heard so many troops in other divisions say the same thing. In the five months I was in the trenches, I only once saw one of our Brigade Staff visit us, and not once did any of the Divisional Staff come near us. After a time we dreaded the idea of making attacks, knowing it would mean heavy casualties and failure.[5]

The attitude of the front-line soldiery was also greatly influenced by the nature of the territory in which they were serving. This is particularly important when considering Flanders, where the BEF was based, which was characterised by largely flat ground that proved very susceptible to flooding and, when dug up, created huge problems in terms of drainage. For this reason, the trenches in Flanders were more often than not full of water and shallowly dug, needing to have breastworks constructed above ground level from earth or sandbags in order to provide sufficient protection. As if the natural state of the ground was not bad enough, artillery shells would serve to churn up the mud even more. Reginald Thomas was a junior officer with the 45th Brigade, Royal Field Artillery and recalled his early days of the war on the Western Front as part of the British 8th Division:

> When we were out there it was a lovely autumn, trenches as dry as a bone, everybody happy and no sickness worth talking about. And within a week, a few days, down came the rain and I won't say filled the trenches but the men were right up to their waists in water, literally. Because then there was firing going on, you see, and you couldn't expose yourself out of the trenches.[6]

By the time of the Third Battle of Ypres in autumn 1917, the Flanders area was notorious for its swampy nature and endless seas of mud. But even by mid-December 1914, only a few months since the outbreak of the fighting, conditions in Flanders could be described as atrocious, as confirmed by Graham Williams:

> [The trenches] were very poor indeed. They were very waterlogged and they were only very sketchy and no

> proper dugouts, they were just a kind of recess in the side of the trench. You couldn't make a proper dugout in Flanders because the water level was only about 2 inches below the surface, in any case, so everything was built up with sandbags. But the trenches themselves were very muddy and very wet. And the reason that these particular ones were so wet was because there was a river there … and for some reason or another, I don't know why, it used to flow sometimes in one direction and sometimes in the other… and that overflowed into our trenches so they were always in a state of more or less waterlogged.[7]

Despite the poor condition of the trenches, the landscape around Ypres was in many places still largely unspoiled by war. The battlefields of the First World War had not yet changed into the barren wastelands that characterised later years.

> It looked more or less like normal times. Ploegsteert Wood which was just behind the trenches was really like a wood then. A few of the trees had got a branch chipped off or something like that, the most dense undergrowth there and you could get into the trenches in daylight from the village; and for that reason Ploegsteert was rather a showplace where various generals and politicians and people used to come up to look at the trenches. They used to bring them up there partly because it was a fairly safe part of the line and also because you could get there in daylight. There were pathways through the wood and when we first went there, these paths were just made of rough wood, bits of branches off the trees, so they were very uneven. But before we left they were replaced by proper duckboards everywhere.[8]

Even in the nearby Ploegsteert village, life was surprisingly carrying on in as normal a manner as possible under the circumstances:

> There were several shops ... a decent butcher, a very good confectioner, various general shops and of course umpteen estaminets, they were all doing a roaring trade. We were actually billeted in one for a time and when we were out of the trenches, these people were so trusting that they used to leave all the drinks on the shelf at night and leave a cup there for us to help ourselves and put the money in.[9]

Yet as autumn inevitably turned to winter, conditions began to deteriorate in Flanders, and much of December was characterised by heavy rain and sleet. Low temperatures meant that nights were often frosty, although this was actually welcomed by the troops since it was better than rain, a much worse occurrence which flooded the trenches and reduced the existing minimal shelter afforded to the soldiers. Poor weather led to a corresponding increase in sickness, frostbite and particularly rheumatism, all collectively linked to the regular catch-all affliction of 'trench foot'.

> When it was frosty it was a bit better because instead of being so muddy it was fairly dry. But if it rained it was of course worse than ever, there was mud everywhere then. In the wood, if you stepped off the path you fell into mud, you had to keep to the pathways. But in the trenches we had braziers and things to keep us warm, they weren't too bad.[10]

Between the front-line trenches of the two opposing armies was a strip of ground which came to be regarded by all troops with extreme wariness. This was No Man's Land, claimed as territory by neither side but which would prove a death trap to anybody foolish enough to enter it. With snipers observing any activity, all excursions into the area for the purposes of scouting or repairing defences had therefore to be undertaken at night, under the safer cover of darkness. The size of No Man's Land would vary in width depending on the local terrain and situation. In some sectors the trenches might be dug extremely close together, perhaps even fewer than a hundred yards apart. Sections of front line such as this would allow either side to throw items to each other and communicate easily; in others, the enemy could only be seen at a distance through binoculars. The proximity of the trenches would remain a significant factor in determining the relationships between soldiers on either side.

A number of yards in front of the front-line trenches was a continuous length of barbed-wire defence, sometimes accompanied by further obstacles intended to prevent any undetected approach. Tunnels and routes beneath the barbed wire went out into No Man's Land to saps and observation posts, from where the enemy could be spied upon. Usually the ground between the trenches was eerily quiet and empty during the daytime, as 2nd Lieutenant Paul Campbell of the Royal Artillery recalled:

> I learnt the names of every wood and all the villages, I knew the contours of the hills and the shapes of the lakes in the valley. To see so much and to see nothing. We might have been the only men alive, my two signallers and I. And yet I knew there were thousands of hidden men in front of me … but no one moved, everyone was waiting for the safety of darkness.[11]

Despite the clear dangers associated with No Man's Land and the general lack of activity in it, at least during daylight, the strip of territory was by no means always desolate, as Albert Moren recalled:

> There was a French place just by us, a French farmhouse, you could see the people had left in a hurry. It was in between our lines and there was still the chickens running about in the farmhouse and the back, and animals.[12]

At night it was a different story. Since No Man's Land was effectively territory shared with the enemy, any activity such as reinforcing the defences was necessarily undertaken during the hours of darkness. Both sides faced the same challenges in this regard, often leading to a curious understanding in which each side allowed the other to carry on with their regular chores. Private Harry Ogle was based in the trenches near Ypres during 1915 and would regularly hear the thump of mallets from the direction of the German trenches.

> Of course! That means German wiring. On the principle of 'live and let live' they take advantage of our preoccupation with our own wiring to do theirs ... Work is in full swing, knock over there, answering knock over here like an echo, and no attempt to muffle or disguise the noise.[13]

As the war developed, so too would the German skill in trench construction, with the elaborate concrete structures evident during the Battle of the Somme in July 1916 providing a good example of how experienced they had become by this time. The French preferred a more segmented approach to their front line, with heavily garrisoned trenches alternating with sections that offered relatively poor defence. But trench warfare as practised by each army was basically similar in nature and shared the same advantages and disadvantages.

Life in the trenches for the individual soldier was largely determined by the section of front in which their battalion, comprising some thousand men, spent most of its time. Defences were split into trench bays, up to 30 feet in length, which were manned by a group of soldiers usually under a non-commissioned officer (NCO). Each of these groups was a cohesive social unit which shared food and drink and 'chatted' (in both senses of the word: conversation undertaken while removing the endemic lice – 'chatts' – from each other's clothing).[14] The unit would look after each other's well-being and effectively served as a family or community that encouraged friendship and solidarity, both in battle and out of action. This sense of loyalty was particularly noticeable among the so-called Pals battalions, volunteer recruits originating from the same local area or occupation, and was also encouraged by the sense of honour and long-standing traditions associated with their respective larger regiment. For many veteran soldiers, relationships enjoyed with comrades during the war were so strong that they often extended into peacetime reunions and lifelong friendships. Henry Williamson, who served in the 1/5th Battalion, London Regiment (London Rifle Brigade), was a volunteer soldier as part of the Territorial Force.

> We were brigaded with regulars who wore balaclava helmets and had beards and the whole feeling was one of tremendous comradeship. Those old sweats who were survivors of Mons and Aisne, they had no fear at all and any apprehension we had of going in under fire was soon got rid of in the trenches.[15]

Duty in the trenches was split between infantry battalions. These were moved in and out of the trenches on a regular basis, to ensure that each man had the same opportunity for rest and to make sure that those in the front line were 'fresh' and ready for potential action. It was a regular turnround process about every eight days; as one battalion handed over to the next, the work of improving the trench defences would carry on as before. As already noted, the nature of the ground in Flanders meant that Christmas 1914 would see significant flooding and the resultant drainage problems would take up a large amount of the soldiers' time when in the line.

*

History as well as human nature has proven again and again that people placed in intolerable and unpleasant situations will usually attempt to change things for the better. Those soldiers in the trenches of 1914 certainly made every attempt to control the environment in which they were forced to exist and to make their fighting and living experience as tolerable as possible under the circumstances. Yet only so much could be done to cope with the situation, due to the element of constant danger and possibility of sudden death. This was only worsened by the fact that trench warfare was by no means predictable in the regularity of casualties inflicted. Apart from the sudden spike in casualties which followed large-scale battles, day-to-day existence in the trenches would most commonly be accompanied by the occasional 'unlucky' death from sniping or shelling. Artillery bombardments in the final weeks of 1914 were far from as common as they were later in the war, since at this relatively early stage of the conflict Britain was experiencing something of a shell shortage. The use of shelling was therefore much more selective than it would later become.

Despite, or perhaps because of, the irregular and unpredictable risk of death in the trenches, daily life on the Western Front was largely characterised by boredom and inactivity. Any activity was generally restricted to ensuring that the trench defences were maintained and repaired where necessary, while sniping and occasional shelling constituted the main danger. Small-scale raiding operations were the most common method employed to keep the infantry busy during periods which otherwise would have been marked by inactivity. These usually involved surreptitious night-time excursions towards the enemy's positions in order to seek useful information about their opponents or to inflict minor harm to them, perhaps by lobbing a few bombs. Private Bernard Adams recognised the cynicism felt by many of the troops towards such activity:

> This trench raiding is a strange business. I think the infantry hate it. The major does not believe that even if they succeed in identifying the unit opposite it makes any difference to our plans. There are easier and better ways of spotting a coming offensive. Probably someone high-up and rather out of touch thinks that trench raids will keep the infantry on their toes and 'cultivate the aggressive spirit'. Out in front, they just don't believe that the results justify their casualties, yet they must obey orders – Poor Bloody Infantry![16]

The danger attached to different sectors might vary dramatically. Soldiers came to distinguish between active sectors where shelling and trench raids were a regular feature, and 'cushy' areas which enjoyed a more peaceful way of life. As the war progressed, some locations such as the Ypres Salient would swiftly gain a reputation as being dangerous and busy places to be stationed, yet the early months of the war had yet to see this develop, as Rifleman Graham Williams recalled:

It was very quiet indeed. Most of the time there was nothing doing at all. Most of the casualties were from snipers ... compared with what we had later it was nothing at all, really. The only weapons of course were rifles and machine guns and artillery; there weren't any of the novelties they had later on like bombs and *Minenwerfer* and all those sort of things. So most of the time there was really nothing doing at all. There was no use firing unless there was something to fire at, and most of the time there was nothing to fire at, you just saw the German parapets. Although at night occasionally there was a bit of firing because Verey lights were being sent up by both sides more or less all the time, and as they moved they sort of cast moving shadows of a bush or depression in the ground that could easily be mistaken for a person moving about and a sentry would loose off at that and the sentry near him would think he'd seen something and he would loose off, and the Germans would think we were going to attack and they'd loose off, so gradually it spread all down the line. That was almost called a 'wind up', you'd get two or three of those every night. But during the day there was only a sniper now and then. If anyone was rash enough to show his head above the parapet, ten chances to one he'd get a sniper's bullet somewhere near him, if it didn't get him. But apart from that it was quite quiet and there was very little artillery fire on the trenches. What shells they did send over were mostly in the back areas to try to catch billets or stores or battery positions or something like that. Just now and then they'd send over about half a dozen shrapnel shells over the trenches, but that was about all. So most of the time it was pretty quiet.[17]

Quiet areas of the front were largely dependent on the attitude of the combatants located there, since a shared lack of aggression would encourage the practice of a 'live and let live' mentality. It was still within the power of those in the front line to influence events at a local level, as a certain degree of autonomy remained outside large-scale campaigning. General Hans von Winterfeldt, Supreme Quartermaster of the German Army, reflected on how such a mentality became a standard part of trench life in many sectors of the line:

> It seems like even the enemy is making every effort to keep low, as we barely encounter any of them. It is strangely calm. Between the two lines in the northern sections we even have something like a friendly exchange of good wishes developing.[18]

The idea of 'live and let live' effectively meant a truce in which both sides avoided deliberate offensive action for an agreed period of time. This supposed a complicit agreement from either side to avoid aggression, with one army's desire for peace being reciprocated by the other. Such a situation was often a spontaneous development, connected directly to both sides sharing a general lack of hostility which may sometimes have been linked to collective reasons such as living conditions. Poor weather served to discourage attacks, for instance. At other others times a truce was sometimes agreed upon 'officially' via communication between the two front lines. Such arrangements could exist for a short while, or sometimes continuously for weeks or months. Accounts of armistices enjoyed with the enemy, whether spontaneous or arranged, remain a common feature of many trench memoirs. To give but one example, the following observation was made by an anonymous German soldier and published in 1915:

> The image of war does not always present itself in its raw reality. Since in so many instances there is only a very short

distance separating German and French positions, so much so that one can actually hear one another talk, a proper communication channel developed between the two enemy trenches during the past few months. We would make certain agreements diligently adhered to by both sides and we would arrange for ceasefires at particular set times; we exchanged food, drinks, tobacco and with that there would be moments where a friendly exchange was the name of the game. Mind you, that only took place between French and German. There was not the faintest whiff anywhere of any fraternisation between our troops and those of the Belgians or even the English.[19]

Fraternisation between the British and Germans certainly did happen, though, as we will come to see in greater detail. Yet differences in attitude between the warring nations were obvious, which may in turn have influenced their relationships with their opponents, as the British soldier Graham Greenwell reflected:

With the French, whenever they were in the trenches, absolutely everything was peaceful until the great day came for a proper offensive. They did not believe in annoying the other side. And opposite us we had Saxons, for instance, and you had a peaceful time, exchange pleasantries sometimes at night. 'How's the Savoy?' they sometimes used to say, sort of thing! But on the other hand if you had the Prussian guard in front of you, then you didn't have that sort of thing.[20]

To illustrate the kind of fraternisation which was happening during the first few months of the war, let us examine an account by a German soldier as transcribed by Dr Otto Krack, giving a specific example of communication between the men of his unit and the French troops opposite. Shouted exchanges had already created an atmosphere of conviviality in that particular part of the line, so the Germans discussed among themselves the possibility of arranging a temporary ceasefire. But it would involve making a deal with their enemy.

> I left the trench waving above my head what once was a white handkerchief. Steadily approaching until I was quite close to the French trench, I still couldn't see anybody coming out from their side even though I kept encouraging them to do so. I continually received the response that they couldn't trust the Germans. Finally, I got fed up and slowly turned around. Just before I had reached our positions, I heard a voice behind me calling … so, I turned back again and walked towards the friendly enemy. Slowly, cautiously, a very tall lieutenant came towards me. We met up at their front trench and greeted each other as if we were old friends. He told me that his commander wished to have a word with me, that he was quite high up in the ranks and that he feared we would trap them by firing at them eventually. I insisted that this high-up gentleman be good enough to come face-to-face with me … Shortly thereafter a 1st lieutenant showed up and he spoke German as he had spent one year in Frankfurt am Main. I then enquired about what it was that he was after, but he simply responded by asking me the same question. I kind of hoped that the whole lot of them would just give themselves up and he likely thought the very same thing. So, we had no other option than to stand there chatting about this and that relating to the war.
>
> The French blamed me for the fact that we Germans had started the war, after which he launched into reporting on the most awful events that had taken place in Belgium. To give this more weight they handed me some copies of *Le*

Matin. I retaliated by notifying them of what the true facts were, accused them of being disturbers of the peace and clarified none too gently that the real criminals were the Belgians. Comrades back in our trenches must have become aware of our exchange of newspapers, as one of my lot arrived carrying a big pile of them which I handed to the 1st lieutenant so that he might read and learn for himself.[21]

This exchange of war news would swiftly be followed by a further trade, to cement the notion of friendship between the two officers:

The lieutenant, meanwhile, preoccupied by what was really important to him, asked yet again for cigarettes, *'Pas de cigars, camarade?'* At which point I sent my corporal out to get him some. We thus took leave, not before assuring one another of our highest mutual respect. But just before setting off, Corporal S. arrived out of breath and carrying a box of cigars. I asked the sergeant to wait, took the box and handed it to him with the words, *'Prenez cette boîte comme cadeau, camarades Allemands.'* ['Take this box as a gift, German comrades']. Well, you should have seen his beaming face! While this fellow made haste with his loot in hand, I returned to our positions at a purposely leisurely pace and received an ecstatic reception from both my comrades and the officers who had rushed to greet me. I had to relay to them the whole story, of course, and submit a report to the chief of the company. And from the 1st lieutenant, I was honoured to receive a very beautiful *Jägerpfeife* [hunter's whistle].[22]

Such ceasefires or truces were by no means uncommon in the early months of the war, as both armies sought to understand the conventions of trench warfare and identify ways in which to make the situation as agreeable as possible. It was perhaps an inevitable consequence of the opponents being stationary in such close proximity to one another, sharing the same living conditions and challenges while not yet totally influenced by the hatred which was largely prevalent back home. That sense of utter disregard towards the enemy would not necessarily manifest itself among the fighting troops until much later in the war. In the meantime, small-scale fraternisation continued to happen from time to time.

The German newspaper *Leipziger Volkszeitung* published a soldier's letter which makes reference to a truce with the French troops opposite, in autumn 1914; although the account is perhaps somewhat exaggerated for comic effect, it does make the point that such truces were by no means unusual:

> All of a sudden, a German lieutenant became aware of a large group of French soldiers sitting on the parapet of the German trench and ordered that they immediately be taken prisoners. His men responded to him, 'That won't be possible, lieutenant, as sixty of our men are sitting over there on the French side.'[23]

Indeed, it should be remembered that truces and fraternisation were not unique to the First World War, having been a standard characteristic of many earlier conflicts. The most recent Boer War had seen numerous examples of ceasefires being called to collect casualties, while during the earlier Napoleonic wars between Britain and France, it was far from unheard of for officers in particular to fraternise with their enemy counterparts between battles, almost as part of a 'gentlemanly' agreement. This notion of officers behaving in a different way to the ordinary troops, almost as if they were enjoying a more civilised understanding with their opposite number, had largely disappeared by the time of the First World War. Yet it is tempting to think that vestiges of this earlier behaviour might have persisted in the minds of both armies.

Of course, not all military units were so open to the possibility of truces or fraternisation. The likelihood of a particular battalion involving itself in a 'live and let live' arrangement might be dependent on that battalion's reputation, for instance, since some regiments enjoyed being regarded as highly obedient and efficient fighting units who would never entertain the idea of friendship with their enemy. Others, however, were only too ready to avoid unnecessary bloodshed. Differences within each nation were apparent, too; first-hand testimony from the trenches largely acknowledges that Saxon Germans were much more likely to be friendly than Prussians. The heritage and history of one's fighting unit might therefore count for a great deal. The regular shift of different units in and out of the front line would also be a deciding factor. If a temporary truce was in place between two opposing units, the situation might often return to normal when one battalion took over from another. The relieved troops might well have mention the unofficial arrangements to their incoming comrades, but sometimes the incoming unit might have a more aggressive attitude that would put an end to any temporary understanding.

Those truces and agreements which did occur throughout this time remained largely small scale in nature, however, and would never last for long. But the fact that fraternisation was far from an unusual phenomenon, as well as the realisation that ceasefires could prove advantageous for specific purposes, would mean that it was only a matter of time before such incidents became more prominent and long-lasting. This existing experience of truces with the enemy would certainly have been remembered by many soldiers as Christmas fast approached.

CHAPTER TWO

Christmas Approaches

Once it became clear that the war would not be over before 1914's celebration of Christmas, many religious leaders were encouraged to make appeals calling for peace to be brokered, even temporarily, in time for the Christian holiday. While history would record the ultimate failure of these calls from 'the top', they do prove interesting when compared to the limited success achieved by those at 'the bottom' – the soldiers in the field. Organised and carefully worded appeals for an armistice would fail, yet spontaneous attempts in certain areas of the Western Front would bear fruit. But it would not be until Christmas itself that the soldiers' wishes for a seasonal truce would properly manifest.

Towards the end of September 1914, Nathan Söderblom, head of the Lutheran Church in Sweden and recipient some years later of the Nobel Peace Prize, became one of the most notable voices to oppose the war when he called on all Christian leaders around the world to work for peace and justice. He argued that the political differences between warring nations should be recognised as unimportant when compared to the Christian brotherhood existing between them.

> Unbearable pain comes in the wake of the world war. The Church, the Body of Christ bleeds from the piercing wounds. The people cry out in their moment of need: 'Lord, how much longer, how much longer?' History will reveal what were the final, true causes of this war, and how they multiplied over time. History may also uncover

the decisive blow to rupture the peace. The Lord knows what makes the heart beat and He passes judgement on hidden thoughts. We are mere servants of the Church, and we appeal to all those who yield power and have influence on dealing with these matters – we wish to impress upon them to consider peace seriously, so that soon there will no longer be any shedding of blood. We would especially like to call on our Christian brothers and sisters, spread across all the different countries around the world, and remind them that war cannot sever the ties by which we are, through Christ, linked together, one tied to the other ... Indeed, what our eyes fail to see and what they fail to recognise, our faith may yet be able to see clearly: that warring between people must submit to the dominion of God, that all Christian believers should be united.[1]

There were many such initiatives for some form of ceasefire which circulated in the run-up to Christmas that year. An 'Open Christmas Letter' asking for peace and addressed to the women of Germany and Austria was written and signed by over a hundred British suffragettes before the end of December:

The Christmas message sounds like mockery to a world at war, but those of us who wished and still wish for peace may surely offer a solemn greeting to such of you who feel as we do. Do not let us forget that our very anguish unites us, that we are passing together through the same experiences of pain and grief ... Though our sons are sent to slay each other, and our hearts are torn by the cruelty of this fate, yet through pain supreme we will be true to our common womanhood ... Do you not feel with us that the vast slaughter in our opposing armies is a stain on civilization and Christianity, and that still deeper horror is aroused at the thought of those innocent victims, the countless women, children, babes, old and sick, pursued by famine, disease and death in the devastated areas, both East and West? ... Can we sit still and let the helpless die in their thousands, as die they must – unless we rouse ourselves in the name of Humanity to save them? There is but one way to do this. We must all urge that peace be made with appeal to Wisdom and Reason ... May Christmas hasten that day.[2]

Sent immediately before Christmas and published widely shortly thereafter, the strong message would elicit a sympathetic response from a great number of the authors' German and Austrian counterparts. Yet the most significant achievement of the letter was arguably more to strengthen the shared goal of women's suffrage rather than bringing an end to the war closer.

The Roman Catholic Church contributed to the religious calls for peace in the approach to Christmas through an appeal by Pope Benedict XV for 'brotherly love'; fraternal sentiments should prevail, emphasising the shared values among nations and the mutual suffering which each was experiencing. Europe's statesmen largely chose to ignore the Pope's encyclical of 1 November appealing for peace, perhaps due to the perceived ambiguity of the Church's diplomatic stance. Which side was the Holy See really supporting in the war? Each nation felt that it was conducting war on the side of 'right', with German Prussian soldiers famously going so far as to have the rallying cry *'Gott mit Uns'* ('God with us') inscribed on their uniform belt buckles. Although the Church strove to raise itself above both warring factions, preferring to emphasise the humanitarian concerns involved, any attempts by it to push the cause of peace were largely ignored by those in power. Indeed, a Staff major in the British Army, Lord

Douglas Loch, chose to question the Papal entreaty directly in a letter home dated 13 December:

> What truth is there in the Pope proposing an armistice for Christmas? If true and accepted I don't think hostilities will be resumed – I don't think it ought to be accepted – We are out here for war and this cannot be mixed up with 'Peace on Earth ... good will towards men'. War is a brutal and loathsome business and the soonest way to end it is to make war with guns whole heart and soul regardless of cost and regardless of all the amenities of peacetime.[3]

Recognising that the opportunity had now passed for a realistic implementation of peace before Christmas, the Pope issued a final such appeal on 24 December in a speech to the College of Cardinals. His oration was, quite unknowingly, delivered at exactly the same time that the first instances of fraternisation were beginning to take place on the Western Front:

> We have made every effort both publicly and in person, privately, to consider any advice, any offer and any desire to make peace. To this end, we attempted to break through the darkness that is war and death so at least one ray can shine through, one ray of the divine peace, a brief and delineated Christmas truce. Albeit aware that we are unable to dispel the black ghost of the war, we might at least alleviate the painful wounds it inflicts. Oh! The dear hope that we had conceived of consoling many mothers and brides with the certainty that, in the few hours devoted to the memory of Divine Christmas, their loved ones would not fall victim to the sword of the enemy. Oh! The sweet illusion of returning to the world at least a taste peace which for so many months has been evading us! Unfortunately, our Christian initiative

was not crowned with happy success. But not for this reason discouraged, we intend to continue every effort to hasten the end of the incomparable disaster, or to alleviate at least the sad consequences.[4]

Just as those at home were thinking about the coming Christmas celebration, the thoughts of many soldiers at the front would have been drawn towards the realisation that they would be experiencing Christmas on active service away from their loved ones. For many this would also mean being in the trenches, in positions of direct danger, as far away from a situation of genuine peace and goodwill to others as might be conceived.

By now, both opposing armies had been entrenched for some weeks and were becoming quite accustomed to the different nature of military life. It had soon become clear to those in the front lines that, whether British, German, French or any other nationality, all the soldiers were experiencing much the same challenges in terms of their everyday existence. All shared the same weather with the resultant flooding and mud; the same challenges associated with manning such rudimentary defences; and identical dangers from sniping and shelling. The natural reaction, then, was for the ordinary troops to empathise with one another. The downtrodden 'Poor Bloody Infantry' of one side were no different to those from the other.

It was largely because of this increasing empathy between the front lines that the end of November and beginning of December were marked by some particularly notable instances of communication between the opposing troops. As already mentioned, in some sectors of Flanders the trenches were relatively close together, which encouraged easy communication. On 17 November the 1st Battalion, King's Own Scottish Borderers, reported that the Germans opposite them were heard to be singing and clapping, although there was no let-up in the British rifle fire. By 30 November, their brigade war diary made a further report:

> A certain amount of promiscuous shelling today ... Enemy's 'pop gun' has been firing all day off and on into Essex area, apparently aimed at nothing ... Semaphore communication established with enemy, but his signallers are so bad that their replies cannot be read. Germans report verbally that they are being relieved and going back for a fortnight's rest.[5]

By now the King's Own Scottish Borderers had been relieved by the 2nd Battalion, Lancashire Fusiliers, who appear to have been more open to the possibility of communication with the Germans. The following day, it seems that German expressions of friendship were being reciprocated by the British.

> Lancashire Fusiliers are offering Germans bully beef in exchange for helmet badges and bargain is complete except for a slight disagreement as to who should come out of his trench first to fetch his share ... There is no doubt the Germans in front of Essex have been relieved by rather a surly lot. They will not answer when spoken to. In front of the Lancashire Fusiliers they do not appear to have been relieved.[6]

As commander of the British II Corps, General Sir Horace Smith-Dorrien was soon made aware of such behaviour and issued orders on 5 December which were intended to draw attention to such relaxed practices and eradicate any possibility of their repeat. What is particularly interesting to note in Smith-Dorrien's orders is not so much his criticism of fraternisation, which is quite understandable from the point of view of a senior commander, but rather his acceptance that the situation demanded sympathy. Like the majority of high-ranking officers in the British Army at that time, Smith-Dorrien was a veteran of the Anglo-Zulu and Boer Wars. His own military experience perhaps reminded him of the dangers involved when troops experienced boredom rather than having the opportunity to practise aggression.

> Experience of this and every other war proves undoubtedly that troops in trenches in close proximity to the enemy slide very easily, if permitted to do so, into a 'live and let live' theory of life. Understandings – amounting almost to unofficial armistices – grow up between our troops and the enemy, with a view to making life easier, until the sole object of war becomes obscured, and officers and men sink into a military lethargy from which it is difficult to arouse them when the moment for great sacrifices again arises. The attitude of our troops can be readily understood and to a certain extent commands sympathy. So long as they know that no general advance is intended, they fail to see any object in undertaking small enterprises of no permanent utility, certain to result in some loss of life, and likely to provoke reprisals. Such an attitude is, however, most dangerous, for it discourages initiative in commanders, and destroys the offensive spirit in all ranks. The Corps Commander, therefore, directs Divisional Commanders to impress on all subordinate commanders the absolute necessity of encouraging the offensive spirit of the troops, while on the defensive, by every means in their power. Friendly intercourse with the enemy, unofficial armistices (e.g. 'we won't fire if you don't', etc.) and the exchange of tobacco and other comforts, however tempting and occasionally amusing they may be, are absolutely prohibited.[7]

Perhaps surprisingly, considering the clarity of this message from the corps commander, a further incident of fraternisation was soon being reported nearby in the same sector on 11 December, this time by the 2nd Battalion, Essex Regiment:

> [At] 10am officers and men of A and D Companies meet Germans half way between the trenches. Germans say they were fed up. Regiment occupying trenches 181st Regiment of 19th Saxon Corps. Trenches appeared to be held in about same strength as ourselves and in same state.[8]

The official response from higher up followed two days later. Brigadier General Frederick Anley, in command of the 12th Infantry Brigade, issued orders to remind his men of the earlier instructions from their corps commander and sternly forbid any further communication or fraternisation. This would be reinforced by the opening of a barrage of heavy fire on the Germans twice that same day. But in many ways the reminder proved unnecessary, since in only a few days' time the brigade would be heavily involved in the final British offensive of the year. Indeed, just as many soldiers would be considering ways of making their imminent Christmas in the trenches as tolerable as possible, their commanders were in the stages of planning the new offensive that would seek to take advantage of the situation before the increasingly wintry conditions made any further attacks impossible.

*

The British offensive on the Western Front in December was based on a series of partial attacks, hastily arranged in order to support the much larger French assault launched elsewhere along the line which had been designed in part on the basis of intelligence indicating that several German detachments had been transferred east. As the larger force, the French would attack along a wide section of front reaching south to the Aisne and the Vosges region. The BEF based in Flanders would attack all along its existing front line, having particular responsibility for the capture of the towns of Messines and Warneton, with the aim of driving the enemy from its position on the left bank of the river Lys.

With hindsight, the British action was doomed to fail from the very start due to the absence of a single coordinated push. Instead, each division would attack independently but in an ongoing sequence, with the opening battle beginning on 14 December. Corporal George Cleghorn of the Gordon Highlanders was involved in this initial assault and afterwards wrote home to his family to describe the experience. As for many other soldiers freshly arrived on the Western Front, it was his first taste of proper fighting.

> I have just come from the trenches where I had my first baptism of fire. I will never forget it. The Gordons and Royal Scots had to take some trenches. This they did, but at some loss. In this my first ordeal under fire the noise did not trouble me, nor the shells, but when I saw my mates knocked over I felt a bit giddy. But this passes away, and it becomes part of the day's work. The ground was in an awful state. We were up to the knees in mud and water, shivering with cold.[9]

Although the French Battle of Artois would continue into the New Year, with a second French assault launched on 20 December in the Champagne region further south carrying on for another three months, any significant British involvement in the offensive concluded by 19 December. Their entire attack had failed to result in any significant gains, having been poorly planned and conducted in a piecemeal way on ground unsuitable for effective fighting. The British assault on Wytschaete, carried out by two infantry battalions on 14 December, suffered from a lack of artillery support and led to hundreds of casualties, while the action four days later at Ploegsteert Wood saw many soldiers hit by their own artillery fire before they had even reached the enemy lines. While some ground was successfully captured by the 2nd Battalion, Devonshire Regiment, a German counter-attack the following morning swiftly restored the status quo. The final assault was made on 19 December near Givenchy, by Indian troops from the Meerut and Lahore Divisions of the Indian Corps. The fighting in this sector would continue in fits and starts until Christmas Eve, but with only minor gains in return for heavy casualties.

The failure of these December attacks proved extremely pertinent to the events that would transpire over Christmas, only a few days later. Many dead and fatally wounded soldiers from both sides lay out in the open in No Man's Land, scattered between the trenches, with their recovery made very difficult due to regular sniping. The desire to remove these fallen comrades from the battlefield for both practical and ethical reasons would have been uppermost in the minds of the British, French and Germans. Indeed, almost immediately after the fighting came to a close, some local unofficial armistices were established in order to deal with these bodies, as Lieutenant Geoffrey Heinekey of the 2nd Battalion, The Queen's Royal Regiment, wrote to his mother:

> The next morning [19 December] a most extraordinary thing happened – I should think one of the most curious things in the war. Some Germans came out and held up their hands and began to take in some of our wounded and so we ourselves immediately got out of the trenches and

began bringing in our wounded also. The Germans then beckoned to us and a lot of us went over and talked to them and they helped us to bury our dead. This lasted the whole morning and I talked to several of them and I must say they seemed extraordinarily fine men ... It seemed too ironical for words. There, the night before we had been having a terrific battle and the morning after, there we were smoking their cigarettes and they smoking ours.[10]

Although, as we have already noted, such armistices were not unheard of on the Western Front during the final months of 1914, the circumstances of this particular one, as well as a similar ceasefire held opposite the sector occupied by the 2nd Battalion, Scots Guards, are remarkably similar to those that would occur in greater number at Christmas time. Having the additional elements of fraternisation between the troops and the exchange of conversation and cigarettes, these incidents do seem very much like a definite dry run for the Christmas Truce proper.

However, one notable difference between the 19 December armistice and the later Christmas ones is not least the fact that while the Christmas Truce would largely prove to be relatively long-lasting and well understood from the perspectives of both sides, this one was extremely ad hoc. Perhaps as a result of this lack of a cohesive understanding between the two sides, or maybe because of the localised nature of the ceasefire, the event involved a number of fatalities. At least one British officer and a private soldier were shot (allegedly by Germans in the adjacent sectors), while two other officers and seven stretcher-bearers were taken prisoner after approaching too near to the German trenches. One of these officers was 2nd Lieutenant Charles Gardner Rought of The Queen's (Royal West Surrey Regiment), who was collecting bodies from No Man's Land.

I was now standing close to a sap, running from the advanced trench to the main firing line, and started to move off to lift one of our fellows who was lying close by. Several of our NCOs and men were by this time hard at work amongst Germans, who were also helping to rescue the wounded – but the German officer caught my arm and said I was not to go. For a moment I remonstrated and after saying something in German, the officer said, 'War is war.' I made some remark in which I used the word 'treachery', whereupon I was pulled by some soldiers, evidently by command of their officer, into their sap and drawn into their main trench. The officer, holding a revolver to my chest, said that if I repeated my remarks he would shoot me. He cooled somewhat and stated that I must see his commandant and with his permission might return to my own lines, but as I had seen their position he must keep me. It was now I noticed Lieutenant Walmsley and saw the Germans taking his equipment from him. He was about 20 yards distant and they brought him and one or two men and sent us down their trench under escort. As we passed, away to our left we could still see Germans mixed up with our men attending to the wounded in No Man's Land.[11]

The whole ceasefire ended abruptly once the British artillery, presumably unaware of what was going on in No Man's Land, happened to open fire on the enemy trenches. Charles Rought would spend the rest of the war as a prisoner in German captivity. He was an interesting character, having won a silver medal on behalf of Britain for his rowing exploits in the 1912 Olympics; having survived captivity, he was awaiting demobilisation back in England in January 1919 when he died in tragic circumstances after eating a bad oyster.

With the final offensive of the year now over for the British at least, the occupants of the Flanders trenches could turn their minds to the imminent celebration of Christmas. Just as with a traditional Christmas celebrated at home, much of the work and preparation for the seasonal merriment was achieved in the days and weeks before Christmas Day itself. A desire to recognise Christmas was common to all combatants. Indeed, many of the key traditional elements – such as the evergreen tree and Yule log, exchanges of presents and the character of Santa Claus – had German origins, despite being long-standing customs enjoyed by all of the different European cultures present on the Western Front. Christmas was always a shared celebration, in the way that other national celebrations were not – the French might celebrate their Independence Day on 4 July with a particularly strong artillery bombardment, for instance, as would the British for their patriotic St George's Day. The Germans would often use the Kaiser's birthday as an excuse for singing and celebrating on 27 January, while many Indian soldiers would celebrate the annual festival of light, Diwali. But whatever faith they might follow, an understanding of the holiday nature of Christmas was shared by all.

Soldiers' feelings of separation meant that a great emphasis was already being placed on the importance of maintaining a regular supply of mail between those at the front and loved ones back home. By the end of 1914, hundreds of thousands of letters were being sent from home to those on active service at an estimated rate of around 2,500 each day. With 12 December announced as the last posting date before Christmas, that week saw 200,000 parcels dispatched from Britain to the troops on the Western Front. A national desire to contribute to soldiers' well-being meant that as Christmas approached, the newspapers and magazines of all combatant nations exhorted the public to remember those at the front by contributing to charitable appeals. These might be in the form of maintaining a 'pen pal' correspondence with soldiers (something that proved a particularly popular pastime among schoolchildren), or contributing to charitable appeals to supply the troops with comforts in the way of food, clothing or Christmas treats. Germany organised *Liebesgaben* gift parcels to be sent to its forces at Christmas time, containing items such as books, tobacco, soap and chocolate. The authorities also collaborated with schools and other organisations to encourage girls to sew and knit items of warm clothing to help their soldiery during the cold weather. Crown Prince Wilhelm recalled this generosity in his memoir of 1923:

> Our first Christmas celebrations in the field! It brought our faithful fighters a most extravagant outpouring of charitable gifts which had flooded in from a thankful and compassionate homeland. Countless war letters replete with inspiring thoughts document the building of bridges between the Christmas celebrations in the dugouts and huts on the one hand and the more beautiful festivities observed back at home.[12]

Aware of the need to set an example for others to follow, the royal families of both Britain and Germany established their own charitable missions. The Duke of Württemberg provided gifts to his German Fourth Army in the form of cigarettes accompanied by a personal photograph, while Crown Prince Wilhelm sent a commemorative pipe to each of his troops, bearing his royal personage. In Britain, King George V's 17-year-old daughter Princess Mary launched an appeal which resulted in the distribution of a brass tin (made from silver in the case of officers) to every serviceman at Christmas time, containing a greetings card from Mary and her photograph, as well as tobacco, sweets or writing equipment. Around 400,000 would be delivered in time for Christmas. The large number of such tins still extant in museum archives and personal collections indicates how valued such gifts were to the soldiers in the field, who felt compelled to keep them safe and send them home as wartime souvenirs. Indeed, the distribution of gifts and mail from home had an almost ceremonial importance to the troops, as this diary entry by Hans Meisner from Baden suggests:

> Our company therefore gathered on the evening of the 23rd at around 6pm in a brewery where two Christmas trees had been put up in the cellar. Our lieutenant made a speech and one could notice a tear or two running down the cheeks of our bearded fighters. Christmas presents were handed out which our loved ones had sent to us from home, among other things we received a whole crate of gingerbread and another one filled with *Springerle* [biscuits] both donated by the Grand Duke and Duchess. We also had mulled wine. After a very pleasant evening, the celebration was cut short at 8pm and two hours later the company marched back to our fortification. I had returned at 8.30pm to my area where we had put up and decorated our own Christmas tree. Under the glow of the candles I opened my own little Christmas parcel I had received from my family, though I had already opened at lunchtime those that had come from Aunt Rosa and Grandmother. I then put out the candles so I could reignite them the next day.[13]

One of the most interesting German accounts of celebrating Christmas in 1914 comes from Otto Hahn, already an internationally renowned scientist who had been nominated for a Nobel Prize on account of his discovery of radioactive isotopes. He would win the Nobel Prize for

CHRISTMAS APPROACHES

Chemistry in 1944 for his joint discovery with others of nuclear fission. But in 1914 the 35-year-old Hahn, serving as an army officer based at Warneton, wrote home to his wife Edith to tell her about the manner in which his unit was spending Christmas in the line:

> Admittedly, the festivities I had organized for 4.30pm mainly consisted of the distribution of woollen items, charitable gifts all of them, which all troops seemed to be receiving in large quantities. But I made sure to have a separate small present for each of the sergeants and the privates: chocolate, coffee cubes, tea tables etc. – all of which I myself had plenty of and no longer needed so much. For the evening I gave my men permission to brew themselves grog; I paid out of my own pocket and purchased twelve bottles of rum in Lille, of which half already was consumed yesterday. So we will have some more grog ready for those who come out of the trenches today and there will also be some small gifts prepared for them ... every single man in our unit has received a packet on top of the wool parcel, which contained at least one shirt, one pair of underpants, two pairs of socks and other stuff. We actually have a whole bag filled to the brim with woollen garments and apparently there is still so much more left behind at Messines that nobody in our battalion feels they want to bother with picking it up. It has to be said that people in Germany have truly been looking after us splendidly. I often think that one could actually put part of what we've received to very good use in Germany proper.[14]

The good intentions of those at home were not always so appreciated by the troops at the front. Captain Walther Stennes of the 16th (3rd Westphalian) Infantry Regiment complained about the contents of the parcels received by troops, which he felt contained inferior cigarettes, poor chocolate and rarely any useful woollen items:

> I know of people who literally congratulated each other for remaining put in the trenches on Christmas Eve rather than choosing to stand in front of the half-truths represented by the Christmas tree. That whole sorry business of charity-mongers bragging about donating gifts and pushing themselves into the limelight announcing their benevolence seems unpleasant and despicable to one who finds himself in the war zone and it really makes you feel sick to your stomach.[15]

For most troops in the field, however, Christmas did present an opportunity to bring a certain amount of happiness to the usual drudgery of life in the trenches. An important element of Christmas celebrations has always been the aspect of decorating one's home for the season, whether by hanging colourful garlands or displaying a decorated evergreen tree. As already mentioned, Germany had led the way in traditions such as the Christmas tree. Queen Victoria's marriage to the Saxon Prince Albert meant that many German customs began to have a large influence on British celebrations of the season, so that by 1914 the idea of decorating a tree was a well-established one. In these early days of trench warfare, there were many trees still available near the front to be cut down and dressed for the season. No doubt some enterprising soldiers may have found a source for some mistletoe as well, encouraged by the possibility of pursuing local French girls for a traditional Christmas kiss. But as usual the Germans were ahead of the game, since every unit in their armed forces would be sent their own Christmas tree – even including, perhaps surprisingly, the nation's U-boat fleet.

The importance of Christmas trees to the German soldiers in their trenches was apparent to the writer and poet Richard Dehmel, who volunteered for military service at the age of 51 and was serving with the 31st Infantry Regiment at the time that he celebrated Christmas 1914.

> I trudged through the trench in my role as Father Christmas and allowed every man of my train to reach into my sack and help themselves to *Pfefferkuchen* [ginger cake] and chocolates. We lit the Christmas tree at 8pm. The sky was clear with bright stars and the moon shining down on us but there was a sharp wind blowing and it took us over ten minutes to get all the candles lit up at the same time. Then we played the *Präsentiermarsch* accompanied by drums, whistles and a harmonica and sang our old melodies. Lieutenant H. decided to shoot flares into the night before every song and while at the very beginning this was met by a few odd shots from the other side, these quickly subsided. Once we sang *'O du fröhliche, o du selige'* (the Frenchmen knew *'O Sanctissima'*), the men on the other side quietly listened and we thus continued undisturbed with *'Stille Nacht, Heilige Nacht'*, *'Es ist ein Ros entsprungen'*, *'O Tannenbaum, O Tannenbaum'*. And it was only at the very end, when we chanted the Dutch 'We Gather Together', that they shot across a few salvos. But then, when we didn't react to these but simply continued with our recitals, they stopped.
>
> We lifted the Christmas tree over the parapet and eventually the wind blew out the lights. And it should be noted in honour of the enemy that throughout the long celebration not a single gunshot had been fired, though the lit tree certainly would have been a clear and visible target. Even far away, where our neighbouring military corps was embedded, nothing at all disturbed the peace. Still imbued with the Christmas spirit we crawled back into our dugouts

with each small group then lighting its own special tree, paying each other a visit, toasting their loved ones back home who had been so generous to them by sending many gifts and finally simply enjoying the evening as 'the light was still shining'. And when towards midnight we once again lit the large tree in our trench and sang *'Deutschland, Deutschland über Alles'* not a single gunshot was fired from the other side. Praised be the Lord, high above us![16]

The recognisable elements of the decorated tree and carol singing had clearly made an impression on the British troops dug in opposite, in a way that would recur to a much greater extent along other parts of the line on Christmas Eve.

Empathy shared by soldiers of both sides was reflected in the religious nature of the holiday. Regular expression of one's faith was much more common at the beginning of the twentieth century than it is today, with churchgoing remaining an essential part of life back home for many First World War soldiers. Of course Christmas also remained important for those troops who followed non-Christian faiths or were not religious-minded at all, with 25 December remaining a traditional public holiday when it was understood that fun was to be shared with family and friends. Christmas festivities therefore not only provided an easy way for soldiers to express their faith while in the difficult circumstances of the trenches, but also served to remind them of the normal life which they had previously enjoyed and hoped to return to in the future. To enjoy a brief moment of normality within a life now dominated by war and military discipline would be a strong and irresistible antidote to the usual dreariness.

Impromptu religious services were held near the front, while many troops welcomed the singing of carols and traditional military songs. Perhaps it was the powerful sentiments conjured up by singing that encouraged thoughts of comradeship and those at home more than anything else, as a volunteer from Westphalia suggested in his diary:

> Moved by the sanctity of the moment, a small group of our comrades spontaneously broke into song, chanting one of our traditional melodies ... Their heartfelt singing succeeded to stir up emotions and soften even the most unbending of hearts.[17]

Christmas encouraged the notion of sharing and community spirit, although of course these were already strong elements of military life. The closeness of the soldiers in the trenches to their enemy served to emphasise such shared values too. In a letter written home to his family, the 25-year-old German volunteer soldier 'H.S.' from Giessen described his experience of the holiday:

> The leader of our company had even brought a little tree along which he set up in our tight quarters. First we celebrated just among us, in our company, which was lovely and made a wonderful impression. The large barn, our guns and kitbags lined up against the wall and in the middle the tree with all of us gathering around it. We then had a short service in the church at around 7pm, led by the chaplain of our division, and returned to our own group and lit our small tree. Upon chanting our Christmas songs in this French barn, I noted quite a few damp eyes among our lot which I hadn't expected. This was followed by a short speech given by our valiant and much-respected company leader, with a sort of sermon delivered by a volunteer soldier, a student of theology, straight after which we then

enjoyed a cup of *Glühwein* [mulled wine]. Towards the end of the evening we sang a few more Christmas carols and our sergeant finished it by reciting some poetry. We had feared the same type of attacks on Christmas Day by the French as had been experienced in 1870 – but it all remained peaceful. We spent the entire following day writing thank-you letters, with our Christmas tree dangling from the ceiling – as otherwise there wouldn't have been any space for writing.[18]

Despite all these efforts to celebrate peace and goodwill to all, along with the other traditional notions associated with Christmas time, it would be fair to say that in the run-up to 25 December the war largely carried on as normal for most of its participants. The Anglo-French offensive already discussed was conducted on the Western Front during December, and the Germans were not limiting themselves to remaining on the defensive.

On Wednesday 16 December, the two German battle-cruisers *Derfflinger* and *Von der Tann* bombarded the eastern coast of Britain around Scarborough before moving their guns on to Whitby and Hartlepool. The resulting casualty statistics vary, but at least eighty-six civilians were killed and 424 injured, causing great shock as the war came quite literally to the very doorsteps of civilians in Britain for the first time. On Christmas Eve, the first enemy bomb fell on mainland Britain, dropped at 11am by a German aeroplane over Dover. Fortunately no casualties were inflicted, apart from a rather disgruntled gardener who was blown off his ladder while cutting evergreen branches to decorate his local church. A second German bombing mission appears to have been attempted the following day, on Christmas itself, but the aircraft was spotted over Sheerness and pursued by three British scouts until it fled back across the Channel. With a similar disregard for the importance attached to 25 December, and ironically at the very moment that the Christmas Truce was in full swing on the Western Front, British aircraft of the Royal Naval Air Service were attacking the German Zeppelin sheds at Cuxhaven, on the northern German coast, in a carefully planned raid. Hampered by foggy weather conditions, the raid was not particularly successful but proved to be a fine morale-booster when subsequently reported in the British press.

The important factor which links all of these events is that they were conceived and executed by those away from the trenches. Attitudes towards the enemy were very different for those back home or who were remote from direct contact with the foe. The proximity experienced by trench fighters to their enemy and the empathy generated by sharing the same fighting and living conditions, on the other hand, ensured that attitudes were rather different in the front line. When combining this with the annual tradition of Christmas, any opportunity for a relaxation of the usual aggression was at its most likely. Indeed, as Christmas fast approached, the majority of troops on the Western Front would have hoped for a quiet few days in the trenches in order to celebrate the season as best they could, without any undue violence. The luckiest ones were those expectant of a period of leave behind the lines, which would have removed the immediate threat of danger almost completely. Rifleman Graham Williams served with the 1/5th Battalion, London Regiment (London Rifle Brigade):

> We expected to be out of the trenches for Christmas because just before that we'd been in the trenches, we'd come out and done fatigues in Ploegsteert Wood helping the Royal Engineers build various breastworks and things, and we all imagined that was going to continue over Christmas. And we had made arrangements with different estaminets

and places to fix up a Christmas dinner there, for them to provide a chicken or something of the sort and we'd provide all the things from our parcels, Christmas puddings and mince pies and so forth. But on December 23rd, a day before Christmas Eve, we suddenly found that each London Rifle Brigade company, each of the four companies, had then been firmly attached to one of the four regular battalions. Our company, No. 2 Company or B Company, were attached to the Somerset Light Infantry and we were also informed that we would relieve them that evening. So we thought 'Bang goes our Christmas'. We were rather fed up about that.[19]

One company of the 16th Bavarian Reserve Regiment, located in Flanders opposite the British II Corps, also looked forward to the coming festivities and a potential respite from the regular shelling:

> For several days we have been fired at relentlessly, shells ploughing into the ground all around us, it is unbearably cold and we have spent eight nights sleeping in the cellar. What an awful war. Tomorrow is Christmas Eve – it is calm and we are full of nostalgia.[20]

Nostalgic thoughts concerning loved ones back home and the normal civilian existence which soldiers experienced prior to the war were common, and only accentuated by the coming Christmas revelry. Christmas served as a painful reminder of what the troops were missing out on, and despite their various attempts to make the best of a bad situation, it was painfully obvious that a Christmas spent in the front line was no substitute for being back home with family, sharing decent food and drink, and enjoying a warm comfortable bed. Early on in the war, most of those deployed were of an older generation, being fathers and husbands – men who remembered and cherished a Christmas celebrated in the warmth of their families. The German student Karl Aldag wrote home to his family on 18 December from near the town of Fournes, halfway between Armentières and La Bassée:

> This year, Christmas curiously stands in stark contradiction to the gospel of love – and yet, it will surely spread more love than in any other year. Love for your own people and love for God. I feel certain that Christmas is being celebrated this year with more devotion than ever before and will thus be a blessing to many, despite the war. I sang our hymns with sweet joy and deep devotion. We sing them in two parts in our quarters, which in fact is a cowshed with a Christmas tree that someone had adeptly appropriated for our group and which now adorns the only table we have. As if I had been listening to a sermon, both the secret of redemption and the miracle of the birth of God's son were revealed to me ... I truly have faith in the future and this conviction which we all share out here in the field might give us strength and support us in our Christmas celebration. I am writing this in the morning under the light of a burning candle at the table in the cowshed. Comrades straggle in and wash, their straw beds having been left untouched. We had to spend the night on high alert, all packed and fully armed which generally is quite uncomfortable. But throughout the night there was heavy shelling. On the horizon we see large fires with smoke rising up to the sky and in six days it will be Christmas.[21]

Aldag would have found it incredible to learn that in only a few days he, along with many other German soldiers, would find themselves talking and laughing with their British enemy. The first true steps towards establishing such an unusual relationship between foes on the Western Front would be made as Christmas finally arrived.

CHAPTER THREE

Christmas Eve in the British Sector

As Christmas arrived, so too did a change in the weather. While December on the Western Front had largely been characterised by constant rain which caused regular flooding of the trenches, the temperature now began to drop enough to bring a hard frost and the occasional snowfall. This onset of wintry weather was noted by Crown Prince Wilhelm, who was present in Flanders:

> A benign weather God looked after us. After weeks of the most horrible rain a seasonal wintry frost settled, paving a smooth path that stretched across the endless and muddy fields all the way to the comrades in the neighbouring trenches. This change was greatly appreciated by those in the trenches, since frozen ground and snow was infinitely preferable to mud and waterlogged conditions.[1]

The first indications of a temporary, locally arranged ceasefire that can definitely be linked to Christmas, including attempts by the soldiers to fraternise with each other, appeared on 23 December and involved the 2nd Battalion, The Cameronians. Lieutenant Malcolm Kennedy witnessed what transpired, and recorded the uncertainty initially felt by many of the British troops at the German appeals for friendship:

> One of the men on sentry duty called my attention to the fact that the German troops opposite were clambering out into the open, waving their arms in the air and making friendly gestures in our direction. As they were unarmed

and showed no signs of hostile intention, I was wondering what to do when a message came along from the Company Commander, saying 'Don't shoot, but count them!' This was followed a minute or two later by the appearance of Ferrers himself, who warned me against letting any Germans come too close as it might be only a ruse on their part to enable them to inspect our position at close quarters. Although the temporary truce that followed was apparently a purely spontaneous act of mutual friendship and goodwill, it was of so unique and surprising a nature that it was just as well to take no undue risks. The company on our left, however, allowed a couple of Germans to come across and a friendly exchange of cigars and verbal greetings took place, one of the two Germans jocularly remarking that he hoped the war would end soon, as he wanted to return to his former job as a taxi driver in Birmingham.[2]

Initially only intended (at least by the British) to last for that one day, this particular truce would in fact extend at the insistence of the Germans into Christmas Eve. Interestingly, while the ceasefire arrangement is described in some detail by Lieutenant Kennedy in a private memoir written after the war, there is no reference to it whatsoever in the official unit war diary. Considering the already brief nature of its entries covering the Christmas period, one can only presume that the subaltern tasked with the responsibility of chronicling the battalion's time in the trenches decided that some things were best left unwritten. To fraternise with the enemy was one thing, but to record it in cold written words for history to pass judgement upon was another thing entirely.

In a different part of the line on the same day, some Saxon soldiers of the German XIX Corps were seen to be displaying trees in their trenches, and limited conversation was entered into with the British units located opposite. Officers from both sides negotiated a local truce for Christmas Eve and Christmas Day. Neither of these instances would necessarily have been known to 2nd Lieutenant Spence Sanders of the 1/6th Battalion, Gordon Highlanders, who had freshly arrived in the Bois-Grenier sector front line with his battalion who were part of the 7th Division:

> We left at 11.30pm yesterday [23 December]. At the dressing station a Borderer offered to guide us to our place on their left. He did but when we got there we found it impossible to enter as the German trenches were so close that it wasn't safe to get over the parapet. We about-turned and went along the communication trench. It took us hours to get into position. We had to come through a bad piece of trench with water in it and several men stuck. Spent a rotten night in a miserable little dug-out. This morning [24 December] a man in Number 1 Section was hit in the shoulder – a nasty wound. It quite upset Petrie Hay – he was as white as a sheet and had to have some brandy. The poor devil was suffering badly and will probably have to lie in the trench till night. The German trenches are only about 50 yards away and between are a lot of dead Germans and I believe Borderers, though I haven't seen the latter. The General has just been along to tell us that we must leave an officer and men to mend the wire when we go out. That will be a rotten job for me, I fear.[3]

Similar sentiments were expressed by Graham Williams, who had also grudgingly entered the front-line trenches the day before with his company of the London Rifle Brigade. Making their way to the section of trench allotted to their unit, the conditions underfoot were found to be atrocious:

CHRISTMAS EVE IN THE BRITISH SECTOR

[The] so-called communication trench was absolutely waterlogged, so you couldn't use it, it was liquid mud underneath so we had to go across after daylight. But when we got to the Somerset trench we found that was knee-deep in water and the only dry spot was the fire step and every here and there a sort of little platform built of sandbags which was sleeping accommodation for those off duty. Well ours was the one at the extreme right of the trench, right in the corner, and we'd got a corrugated-iron roof on ours, which was well peppered, so that's where we settled down for the night.

Next morning, Christmas Eve, was a beautiful bright winter's day, cold but very sunny and bright and quite a pleasant day. The only thing which sort of marred it was during breakfast time, a chap in the next bay to us was a very popular young singer in the company, he was shot through the head by a sniper on that morning. And of course in those days, so early in the war, casualties were very few and far between, especially in this sector, so any casualty was something to be talked about in the whole battalion. It was very different later on, of course. Anyway his body was put at the back of the trench to be taken away at night and the day went on as usual, the ordinary job of filling sandbags. I mean that was a job for three men in that part, one to hold the sandbag open, another one to scoop it up with a shovel, and a third one to scrape the sort of glutinous mass off the shovel into the bag. And when you put it into the bag it was semi-liquid and oozed out again almost. But that was just one of the jobs during the day.[4]

Christmas Eve was by all accounts very quiet, although the morning did see some limited artillery action by the British, as Lieutenant Menke of the 15th (2nd Westphalian) Infantry Regiment recalled:

On the afternoon of the 24th the English artillery was in neither a festive nor peaceful mood. On the contrary – they destroyed two public buildings in Le Maisnil and we Germans most certainly had to punish them most severely for this action. But then, once the sun had gone down behind the English line, calm settled in. All wind and weather seemed suspended.[5]

Just as it was getting dark at 6.30pm on Christmas Eve, British General Headquarters sent a message out to all its units, informing them that intelligence reports were suggesting that a German attack might be expected at Christmas or New Year, requiring special vigilance during the period. But the message did not reach the front-line infantry until later in the evening, by which time the first steps towards fraternisation had been made and in some areas the Christmas Truce was well underway. The 4th Division signalling service had already announced that it would only be dealing with priority messages during the night of 25–26 December, and it is therefore tempting to presume that something of a Christmas languor had already begun to make itself known among the troops.

The cold and wintry conditions combined with an atmosphere of stillness and quiet, leading one British soldier to observe that the evening was 'a Christmas card Christmas Eve, white beautiful moonlight, frost on the ground, almost white everywhere'.[6] Having spent much of the day filling sandbags and trying unsuccessfully to reduce the flooding in his trenches, Graham Williams now reported for the evening duty:

> We had to 'stand to' for an hour at dusk always because it was always imagined that was when anyone would attack. Probably it was the last time they'd choose because they

knew everyone would be expecting it. Anyway, we had to do that. Then night sentries were posted, two hours on, four hours off, in groups of three for each bay of the trench. Well, my turn for duty was from 10 to 12 midnight. I was standing there on duty and I was gazing across towards the German parapet, nothing much going on but I thought, 'Well a very different Christmas this is going to be from any I've spent up to now.' I thought about this time at home, we'd have finished putting up all the greenery and holly and stuff, and my father would have just finished making his rum punch which he always did at Christmas, from an old recipe written out by my great-grandfather actually. It was kept in the family Bible of all places. Anyway, I thought, 'My word, I could just do with a swig of that rum punch now,' and feeling pretty miserable altogether.[7]

This quiet moment in Flanders proved to be the transitional phase between war and peace. Albert Moren was a private with the 2nd Battalion, The Queen's (Royal West Surrey Regiment), and on that Christmas Eve experienced what he would later describe as 'one of the highlights of my life':

The artillery stopped firing, it quietened down as though something was brewing. There was no rifle fire and the machine guns, they used to go 'pop pop pop pop' at night right down the line, testing the guns ready for the morning, and there was nothing of that. It was all quiet. It was a really eerie sort of feeling as though something was going to happen. The stillness and quietness of everything, it was really remarkable.[8]

This was the moment when it gradually became apparent to the British soldiers that something unusual was happening across the other side of No Man's Land. As the daylight faded, the German trenches were lit up in several places by lights, which further examination through binoculars would reveal as Christmas trees decorated with lit candles placed on their branches. Among the Germans was the 17-year-old volunteer soldier Eduard Tölke, who was serving with the 55th (6th Westphalian) Infantry Regiment.

> Tentative, hesitant, we sit here in our trenches, at long last our trees along the trenches have been lit. The shining trees could be enjoyed all around us and it truly was a festive sight, all the more so as there was no wind and the evening appeared blissful with its white frost covering the ground. It was a festive night and nobody will likely ever forget it.[9]

Lieutenant Fritz Jung chronicled the similar recollections of Jäger Lüdemann with the 10th Jäger Battalion based near Warneton, just outside Ypres, at Christmas 1914:

> The 4th Company was in their trenches by 9pm. It was a beautiful night with a bright moon shining down. Light frost covered the ground. Only snow was missing in this near-perfect picture of Christmas Eve. But soon a proper Christmas spirit uninterrupted by the English fireworks spread through the trenches. The Jäger had brought along with them their own small Christmas trees which had been either mailed to them from home or had somehow been put together on site. The men decorated them, affixed some candles, lit and put them atop the parapet. Before too long one could see at a furthermost distance and to the left of us, where the Bavarian Jäger were embedded, a whole line of lit trees, and further along the Saxon infantry had put up theirs. It was an unforgettable sight![10]

CHRISTMAS EVE IN THE BRITISH SECTOR

Lieutenant Menke would have agreed with both men as to the extraordinary circumstances in which the Germans found themselves celebrating Christmas:

> It was truly a Holy Night! No shooting could be heard far and wide, not a sound – anywhere. The guns rested. The men did not have to go without a Christmas tree either. There must have been one standing in the middle of every single trench. Stars appeared and glittered in the dark sky, when someone must have brought one of the lit trees and placed it on the parapet. Before too long an entire row of Christmas trees decorated the front line from one end to the other. Where previously death and decay were lurking, this simple sign was indicating a German Christmas celebration commanding 'Peace on Earth'. Apparently, on the following day, English soldiers were heard declaring that the sight of the Christmas trees and hearing the German Christmas carols had overwhelmed them. Despite the glorious Christmas tree lights, a German patrol had been dispatched by the 3rd Battalion and ordered to perform guard duty. But instead of being greeted by the customary bullets, they suddenly heard shouts coming from the English trenches addressing them.[11]

The display of Christmas trees decorated with bright shining lights was soon followed by the beginnings of conversation between the Germans and the British troops opposite. The usual repartee enjoyed by soldiers where the trenches were close enough together to allow shouted exchanges took on a different character from normal; the usual insults and jokes were forgotten in favour of hearty Christmas greetings. Music too appears to have played a vital role in bringing the two sides together. 2nd Lieutenant Mervyn Richardson of the 2nd Battalion,

Royal Welsh Fusiliers, recalled his company enjoying an enthusiastic sing-song with the Germans in the trenches opposite, before they held up a sheet of canvas above the parapet, displaying 'Merry Xmas' to the Germans in large letters, accompanied by a portrait of the Kaiser.[12] 2nd Lieutenant Albert Raynes, who was attached to the 2nd Battalion, Royal Berkshire Regiment, described the beginnings of such fraternisation as it developed in their Neuve Chapelle sector:

> I would not have missed it for anything. Christmas Eve was cold and frosty, with a lovely moon (ideal Christmas Eve). Soon after dark, we heard someone in the German trenches shout, 'Hullo English, a Merry Christmas'. Soon all along the line of the German trenches, we heard 'English, we're friends tonight'. 'Don't shoot, we won't shoot'. We shouted back we would not fire. They then fixed small fires like toy lamps all along the top of their trenches and sat on the parapet. Most of them could speak English and shouted all sorts of things, asked for the latest football results, asked if we would like a song. We shouted back 'yes', whereupon they struck up the 'Watch on the Rhine'. The whole of the German line for a considerable distance took it up, and sang it with great gusto. When they had finished we struck up 'Tipperary', then they sang an Austrian hymn and we replied with 'Rule Britannia'. Several Germans came half-way, but none of our fellows went out to meet them during the night. They became quiet during the night except for an occasional cheer or cry. Not a shot was fired.[13]

The lights and singing combined to encourage an exchange of greetings from each trench to the other opposite, as Graham Williams witnessed while on sentry duty:

> When the Germans started singing *'Stille Nacht, Heilige Nacht'*, I [and] all the other sentries all woke up the other people to come along and see this. What on earth's going on? Then after that they finished their carol so we thought, well, we must retaliate so we sang 'The First Noël'. And after we finished that, they clapped us and they started on *'O Tannenbaum'*, the most miserable sort of dirge-like tune really ... and they sang that and we went on with other carols, first us and then the Germans. And then we started singing 'Come All ye Faithful' and the Germans joined in with that, singing the Latin words *'Adeste Fideles'*. Both together singing that, it seemed rather an unusual thing, two sides singing the same carol in the middle of the war. And so it went on.[14]

The vast majority of accounts of the Christmas Eve singing draw attention to the German soldiers singing 'Silent Night' (*'Stille Nacht, Heilige Nacht'* in German), the popular Christmas carol originally composed in 1818 by the Austrian Franz Xaver Gruber, to words by Joseph Mohr. Despite not necessarily understanding the German words being carried through the cold night air, the British listeners would certainly have been familiar with the popular tune and recognised it, along with the sentiments it conveyed, instantly. Albert Moren was particularly taken by the singing:

> They sang something else before *'Stille Nacht'*, another German hymn or German tune which didn't make an impression, but when they sang *'Stille Nacht'* it absolutely took our breath sort of thing, it was so beautiful. I believe they had a cornet player, I'm not certain but they had a musical instrument of some sort which we couldn't define, but that coming over the air from their trenches on that

moonlight night, it was really a thing I will never forget, really amazing. We also saw some trees lit up. They sang it several times, the Germans, it's one of their most popular carols, and everybody thought how wonderful it was. The British troops on our side all listened intently to it.[15]

Johannes Niemann, of the 133rd (9th Royal Saxon) Infantry Regiment, expressed his amazement at how quickly the atmosphere in the front line had changed, from one of outright war and aggression to one of peace and goodwill. The shared love of singing and the natural human desire to encourage and compete with each other had led to a complete change in attitude.

> While yesterday the trumpeters had belted out the *'Wacht am Rhein'* they seem to have switched (today) to *'Stille Nacht'* … the whole war seems to have sunk into bourgeois bliss, with everyone doing the shake-hands bit. Would it be true to say that suddenly peace had broken out? Soon I found myself in the middle of it all. I didn't know what to do … [it] also took place in the neighbouring regiments. And so it came to pass that war turned into the artistic format of a singing contest and both on this and the other side the warring spirits dissolved into a Christmas spirit.[16]

Ernest Morley, of the 1/16th Battalion, London Regiment (The Queen's Westminster Rifles), was based in the Armentières sector and recorded how the joy of hearing the fine singing from the enemy's trenches actually curtailed a British plan to retaliate in a more violent way:

> We had decided to give the Germans a Christmas present of three carols and five rounds rapid. Accordingly as soon as night fell we started, and the strains of 'While shepherds'

(beautifully rendered by the choir!) came upon the air. We finished that and paused preparatory to giving the second item on the programme. But lo! We heard answering strains arising from their lines. Also they started shouting across to us. Therefore we stopped any hostile operations and commenced to shout back. One of them shouted 'A merry Christmas English, we're not shooting tonight' ... and from that time until we were relieved on Boxing morning at 4 am, not a shot was fired.[17]

Also based near Armentières was Private Harold Startin of the 1st Battalion, Leicestershire Regiment, who nicely summed up the rather unusual situation. Rather than facing each other as soldiers, the troops preferred to team up as choristers.

On Christmas Eve, as we were standing-to, the Germans started to sing Christmas Carols, the first one being 'Holy Night', and then as though a preconceived plan we joined in. There we were, the fighting men of the two forces, who had previously been at one another's throats, joining together having a real Carol Concert.[18]

In many stretches of the line all through the Flanders sector, the Germans sang and the British responded in kind, encouraging them and exchanging pleasantries. In some places, such as where the 2nd Battalion, Seaforth Highlanders, were stationed north of Ploegsteert Wood, the Scotsmen were the ones to initiate the singing, with the Germans then applauding and calling for more. This repartee led to more direct requests to fraternise. Fritz Jung suggested that it was the sense of friendship engendered by the Christmas trees and singing which encouraged the British to make the next move, although it took a while for the Germans in that particular sector to appreciate the true intentions of their opponents.

> Tommy arrived but not with hostile intentions. Their mission was of an entirely friendly nature. From afar – we lay opposite each other at a distance of some 400 metres – we could already hear loud shouts in German that were echoing through the night: 'Comrade, don't shoot,' followed by the words, 'We are your friends.' Our lit trees with the many candles must have moved them to such an extent that they simply ran out of their trenches. Our captain didn't know what to do with himself, pacing through the trenches like a madman. He was firmly convinced that we would be ambushed just as he had always feared we would be and thought that the many shouts he heard were nothing but a trick. We too, it has to be said, were feeling rather strange. We were prepared for anything and everything. The captain immediately gave orders to shoot. Light flares rose to the sky and bullets whizzed across the field in the direction of Tommy. But when the shouting didn't cease, in fact only grew louder, the shooting petered out and then stopped altogether. Our bullets had caused no damage. Without further ado Oberjäger Echte from the 1st Company jumped over the parapet and dashed across to the wire fence to see what in fact was going on. Much to his surprise he could see that a whole group of Englishmen had arrived, all of them unarmed. At that point several more men from our side plucked up their courage and joined in. We shook each other's hands, everything was very friendly, and we started chatting, since Oberjäger Echte speaks fluent English. At that gathering we also exchanged gifts. The English presented us with throw knives, tobacco, and our Oberjäger even got a short pipe. Meanwhile we Germans gave them cigarettes.[19]

In other sectors too, individual soldiers cautiously wandered out into No Man's Land towards the opposite trenches, meeting with their enemies to shake hands and exchange souvenirs. This was still largely done on an individual basis, with no more than a handful of soldiers out on top at any one time. Rather than occurring without the knowledge or permission of the officers, it seems that in most cases the officers were complicit in encouraging the fraternisation or, at the very least, turning a blind eye to it. They could justify any such meetings by ensuring that the official report would emphasise intelligence-gathering as a useful consequence of the endeavour. Some units such as the 2nd Battalion, Scots Guards, arranged for a more formal truce to be held the following day under the clarity of daylight.

> On the night of Christmas Eve, the German trenches opposite those occupied by the battalion at Fromelles were lit up with lanterns and there were sounds of singing. We got into communications with the Germans, who were anxious to arrange an armistice during Christmas. A scout named F Murker went out and met a German patrol and was given a glass of whisky and some cigars, and a message was sent back saying that if we didn't fire at them, they would not fire at us. There was no firing during the night.[20]

Men who until that moment had been sworn enemies were now standing out in the open, expressing friendship towards one another. It was almost as if the troops were drunk with the spirit of Christmas, acting in such a remarkable and completely unexpected way. Carl Mühlegg of the 17th Reserve Infantry Regiment summed up the common feeling, as he reflected on the spontaneity of the event:

> On this side, as on the other, [were] soldiers who hadn't done anything to each other and who, on a personal level, weren't enemies; soldiers who had parents, wives and children at home and who, in the midst of the miraculous holy night, and in the mythical hour of the birth of Christ, offered each other gifts and shook each other's hands in friendship. The night was clear, the sky bedecked by stars and a new moon illuminated by the bright lights flared up on both sides of the front. For me personally they gracefully brightened the Holy Night.[21]

Some units preferred to ignore their opponents' calls for friendship, perhaps uncertain of how to respond to such an unexpected development. In some cases, as Graham Williams recalled, the British were uneasy about making the first step towards any fraternisation and preferred to take the easy option, which was simply to avoid instigating any aggression while the Germans were offering peace.

> After a bit one of the Germans called out, 'Come on Tommy, come over and see us.' So I replied in German, I said, 'No, first come here Fritz.' Anyway, he didn't and nobody took advantage of this at the time, they just called various messages to each other, wished them a happy Christmas and so forth, then after a bit they'd run out of carols, I suppose, and so had we and the lights were all burnt out, they were candles I think they must have been, but they were very clear because there was no wind that night ... and we resumed the ordinary sort of turn of sentry duties on and off all night.[22]

Others sought advice from higher up, as the messages preserved as part of the war diary of the 1st Battalion, Royal Irish Rifles, illustrate:

[Message to Brigade, 8.30pm] Germans have illuminated their trenches, are singing songs and are wishing us a Happy Xmas. Compliments are being exchanged but am nevertheless taking all military precautions. [Brigade reply] It is thought possible that enemy may be contemplating an attack during Xmas or New Year. Special vigilance will be maintained during this period.

[Message to Brigade, 11.45pm] Germans before my regiment state they will not fire until midnight 25/26th unless we fire. No shot has been fired since 8pm. A small party of one company met Germans half way and conversed. 158th Regiment, fine men and well clothed. They gave us a cap and helmet badge and a box of cigars. [Brigade reply at 12.35am] No communication of any sort is to be held with the enemy, nor is he to be allowed to approach our trenches under penalty of fire being opened.[23]

*

While a considerable number of infantry units located in Flanders were enjoying the ceasefire and fraternisation which had broken out spontaneously on Christmas Eve, many other troops did not experience anything at all similar at that time. For them, the night may have proven rather quieter than normal, but otherwise the war carried on in the normal way. Some soldiers, such as the German Karl Aldag, were relieved on Christmas Eve and so only heard the singing of carols in the line before returning to the comparative safety of their billets. Aldag would miss the events that transpired on the following day, Christmas Day itself, but wrote home to his wife of the limited fraternisation that he had experienced. His account is perhaps typical of the attitude and feelings of the average soldier at that time, highlighting how the thoughts of the troops would inevitably return to their loved ones back home:

> Christmas in the field! We have just emerged from our Christmas evening, 24 December, at about 10pm. The English also sang Christmas carols; there was, for example, a splendid quartet. With us as well the songs sounded clear and beautiful and there was barely a shot to be heard. We had decorated the stations with branches from fir trees and some gold tinsel which we had received from home and we tried to do the same with our dugouts. Then, at 10pm another company arrived and we marched to reach the headquarters, some one and a quarter hours away. It's been ages since there has been such a beautiful and clear night and it was calm, peaceful and bright just as it should be at Christmas. Frost began to settle on the fields which spelt the end of the past of mud and filth.
>
> I was thinking a lot about home and regretted that this time round you didn't have a Christmas tree, as it was hard to imagine you without one. It was lovely how we all stood together and the names were called up and parcels were being passed down over our heads; each one of us turned into a child who was celebrating Christmas. We knelt in front of our boxes and rummaged around in the soft glow of the candles, we were all gathered together in the cowshed, the bunks lining the walls filled with straw – this must have been what it was like on the first Christmas. The real celebration took place in the evening. Two large trees had been brought in and were standing on the long tables. Whatever you wished for was spread out, in more than plentiful quantities: woollen goods, tobacco, *Spekulatius* [ginger biscuits], chocolate, sausages – all charitable gifts. Germany had truly been generous towards us! Then the commander of our regiment arrived,

followed by the division chaplain, and after the Christmas story had been beautifully narrated we once again sang our wonderful old carols.[24]

News of what was happening at the front began to trickle back to those troops in reserve or away from the areas directly involved in fraternisation. Christmas Eve had seen the German volunteer Otto Hahn travel to nearby Messines, his journey accompanied by the sounds of shelling and the putrid smell of war. But towards evening, calm descended on the front:

> Not a single gunshot, no cannon was fired, neither from our side, nor from the side of the enemy – all was peaceful and nothing here interrupted the Christmas spirit. Casting our thoughts back to yesterday and to the circumstances we had been facing, the change in atmosphere was astounding. Everything, every single little detail, had been prepared and was ready for the likelihood of an alarm being raised. Each one of us had been instructed to be on full alert.[25]

With almost a degree of reluctance, Hahn proceeded to share with his wife his experience of Christmas Eve. What was happening in scattered sectors across the Western Front seemed to be both wonderfully positive but incredibly wrong at the same time.

> My feeling is that I am not really allowed to tell; I am convinced that our superiors suppress it, but it is true: the soldiers in our trenches celebrated Christmas as well. Who knows how it all started? It was a Bavarian Jäger who started it, after the English had called across 'Merry Christmas' in response to our people having stuck a stick out of the trench with a Christmas tree attached to it. The Bavarian Jäger

crept forwards and peeked into the Englishmen's trenches. Perhaps he only crept forwards a short distance and then the English waved for him to approach. He returned with cigarettes and tobacco. We trusted him; he went back there yet another time, and returned bringing with him several Scottish Highlanders in their short skirts who stopped short of our trenches. Our men approached, walking towards them. Not a single shot was fired. We enjoyed a smoke together, lamps were lined up along the edges of the trenches and soldiers of both sides chatted with one another. We didn't chat only on yesterday evening; it continued today as well. Officers of our regiment went across, soldiers emerged in groups. The war was suspended. The Christmas peace had brought this about.[26]

For those soldiers who remained in the front line, the opportunities for extended ceasefires and fraternisation with their enemy would only persist as Christmas celebrations continued. The peace that had begun on Christmas Eve would become even more pronounced on Christmas Day itself.

CHAPTER FOUR

Christmas Day in the British Sector

WHEN DAWN BROKE ON Christmas Day 1914, the sound of war was still noticeably absent from much of Flanders. As the early morning fog faded away to reveal a cloudless blue sky, the ground could be seen to be covered by glistening white frost. If one hadn't been aware of the thousands of men hidden below ground level in their respective trenches, the frosty scene might have resembled a perfect wintry countryside morning. As the men woke and prepared themselves for the daily routine, sentries changed over and preparations began for breakfast. The thoughts of many soldiers would have rested on their loved ones back home, their children waking to find the presents left for them by Father Christmas while families got ready to celebrate the great day despite the notable absences at their dinner tables. The emotional pangs of separation would have been at an absolute peak.

As we have seen, certain soldiers had already involved themselves in the limited fraternisation experienced the previous afternoon and evening. The ceasefires and exchange of pleasantries which had developed in Flanders on Christmas Eve had in many cases been instigated by the Germans displaying Christmas trees in their trenches, before both sides joined voices to sing carols. Although a degree of face-to-face meeting had certainly happened in the neutral No Man's Land, this was still largely low key and had only really involved a relatively small number of individual soldiers. The fraternisation had come to a natural end with the onset of darkness.

Yet now, as a new day began, a fresh opportunity presented itself for the front-line troops to take advantage of the continued spirit of goodwill in a much greater way. The situation from the previous evening had seen small, local arrangements begin to develop, yet daylight would see these sparks of friendship rekindle themselves and combine into something much bigger.

One of the most interesting aspects of the Christmas Truce, which indeed applies to fraternisation outside the trenches in more general terms, is the fact that in normal times all soldiers treated No Man's Land with a respectful dread. To raise one's head above the trenches, or even to allow the enemy to glimpse movement through a break in the defences, would usually invite instant reprisal in the form of a sniper's bullet. It had therefore been drilled into each soldier during their instruction that to climb out of the trench in the direction of the enemy, or even to show their head above the parapet, would induce immediate death. We have already seen how an unfortunate soldier from the London Rifle Brigade was killed in such a way on Christmas Eve morning, and his body laid at the back of one of the trenches to be carried away for later burial.

The 2nd Battalion, Seaforth Highlanders, were in the trenches near the river Douve and recounted how, once the early morning mist had risen, a locally arranged ceasefire allowed them to walk about in the open without fear of being shot. Unfortunately the business-like nature of the war diary entries fails to expand on how the individual soldiers felt at the novelty of such a situation. To be able to climb out of dark, flooded trenches and enjoy the open space and fresh air once again without fear of immediate death must have been an incredibly odd sensation. A slight hint at the popularity of being out in the open, as well as their continuing sense of caution at the situation, is captured in the reference to how they 'had some trouble in keeping the Germans away from our lines'.[1] The most puzzling question, however, concerns how so many soldiers from both sides ultimately found themselves mingling together in this manner in No Man's Land, out in the open, with the desire to fraternise. Some explanation is offered by Leslie Walkinton, a private with the 1/16th Battalion, London Regiment (The Queen's Westminster Rifles), who went some way to describe how a mutual reluctance to initiate aggression led to the gradual process of both armies coming together:

> We were in the front line, we were about 300 yards from the Germans and … on Christmas Eve we'd been singing carols and this that and the other and the Germans had been doing the same. And we'd been shouting to each other, sometimes rude remarks, more often just joking remarks. Anyway, eventually a German said, 'Tomorrow you no shoot, we no shoot,' and a lot of other shouts were exchanged and all that. The morning came and we didn't shoot and they didn't shoot and so then we began to pop our heads over the side and jump down quickly in case they shot, but they didn't shoot. And then we saw a German standing up waving his arms and we didn't shoot, and so on. So it gradually grew and eventually several people were walking about and nobody was shooting. After a time some bold people walked out in front of their barbed-wire entanglement and finally an Englishman and a German met halfway across No Man's Land and they shook hands and laughed and joked and waved to their companions to come out and join them and we streaked out. It was really rather like a crowd at a football match, you know? People from both sides *streaming* out and we met in No Man's Land and we spent the day there. We swapped cigarettes and we gave them rum and

they gave us cognac and so on, and we exchanged odd little bits of food just like a lot of boys from neighbouring schools. We were a bit guarded about what we said, but couldn't have been friendlier. I don't think we discussed the war itself all that much. I'm quite sure that we didn't say, 'This is silly, let's chuck it altogether,' neither side talked like that at all, we all remained absolutely loyal to our side and it was perfectly clear to both sides that at the end of the day we would go back and start killing each other again.[2]

It is important to note that where fraternisation occurred it was rarely undertaken without due consideration for safety. Surviving first-hand accounts invariably contain reference to an awareness by both sides that they would need to maintain their guard against a potential deterioration in the friendship. It is therefore logical that in some instances the beginnings of establishing a truce necessitated a more formal discussion, arranged under the protection of the white flag. Agreements were often made between officers of the opposing units regarding the length of the truce in their sector and any conditions attached to it that would need to be honoured. Such an arrangement established in one part of the line might often lead to another in the neighbouring stretch of front. On Christmas Eve, for instance, the adjutant of the 2nd Battalion, Scots Guards, witnessed activity opposite the trenches to his left, where the Gordon Highlanders were collecting bodies and digging graves. This inspired him to climb out on top and approach the Germans opposite to ask permission to do the same thing for his own fallen men. The war diary for his battalion recounts in unusual detail the fraternisation between the two sides on Christmas Day:

> Early on Christmas morning a party of Germans, 158 Regiment, came over to our wire fence and a party from

our trenches went out to meet them. They appeared to be most amicable and exchanged souvenirs, cap stars, badges, etc. Our men gave them plum puddings, which they much appreciated. Further down the line we were able to make arrangements to bury the dead who had been killed on December 18–19 and were still lying between the trenches. The Germans brought the bodies to a half way line and we buried them. Detachments of British and Germans formed in line and a German and English chaplain read some prayers alternately. The whole of this was done in great solemnity and reverence. It was heartrending to see some of the chaps one knew so well, and who had started out in such good spirits on 18 December lying there dead, some with terrible wounds due to the explosive action of the high velocity bullet at short range. Captain Taylor's body was found amongst them. His body was carried to the Rue-Petillion where we buried him in our little cemetery.

I talked to several officers and men. One officer, a middle aged man, tall, well set up and good looking, told me that Lieutenant Hon F Hanbury-Tracey had been taken into their trenches very severely wounded. He died after two days in the local hospital and was buried in the German cemetery at Fromelles. He also said that another young officer had been buried. He was fair. We think this would be Lieutenant R Nugent who was reported missing. Captain Paynter gave this officer a scarf and in exchange an orderly presented him with a pair of gloves, and wished to thank him for his kindness. The other officers were rather inclined to be stand-offish and of the burger class. Another officer who could not speak English or French appeared to want to express his feelings, pointed to the dead and reverently said *'les braves'*, which shows that the Germans do think something of the British Army.

The men I spoke to were less reticent. They appeared generally tired of fighting, and wanted to get back to their various employments. Some lived in England. One man told me he had been seven years in England and was married last March. Another said he had a girl who lived in Suffolk and said it had been impossible to communicate with her through Germany since war began. Their general opinion of the war was as follows. France is on her last legs and will soon have to give up. Russia has had a tremendous defeat in Poland and will soon be ready to make terms of peace. England is the nut which still has to be cracked but with France and Russia out of the way she, Germany, would be too powerful. The war they thought might be over by the end of January. This shows what lies are circulated amongst the German troops and the hatred which exists between Germany and England.

Discipline in the German Army is of the most rigid character. The men seemed to hate their officers but nevertheless are afraid of them. A photo was taken by Lieutenant Swinton of a group of Germans and English. Both sides have played the game and I know that this regiment anyhow has learnt to trust an Englishman's word.[3]

Some units, such as the 2nd Battalion, Royal Berkshire Regiment, who were in the trenches at Fauquissart, had enjoyed an informal truce with their enemy since Christmas Eve, hastily arranged by vocal exchanges shouted across to each other. But in this case the officers clearly began to get cold feet about the idea of actual fraternisation and therefore took actions to curb the excesses of the situation, while still embracing the opportunity to take advantage of a ceasefire:

Men got up on parapet and advanced half way towards German trenches, and in some cases conversed with them. Orders given at 11am prohibiting men from going beyond parapet. Much work done in improving trenches during this day, the enemy protested against barbed wire being repaired, and we stopped enemy from repairing theirs.[4]

*

For some, the meetings which had begun the previous day simply carried on to a greater extent. Music and singing had often continued intermittently throughout the night anyway, with the darkness and festive atmosphere of Christmas perhaps serving to encourage mindful reflection on those back home. One German account reinforces the importance of music in encouraging both sides to seek an armistice:

> All of a sudden, towards 4am we could hear music ringing through the early morning, floating in from the Saxon trench where they had formed a band that was playing the most beautiful Christmas carols. Surely, every comrade's heart must have melted at the sound of those familiar melodies from our homeland. Each song was received with loud shouts of 'Hurrah!' coming from the English side. There too it eventually quietened down, dawn broke and all around us was peaceful. We could take walks outside without a worry in the world and for the first time we were able actually to roam around the area, taking it all in, while usually we weren't allowed even for a moment to put our head above the parapet for fear of being targeted by English sharpshooters. We also used the time to fix our parapet and anything else which needed mending. Tommy on the other side did the same. Above all we needed to bury the dead who were still lying in the field – most of them were Russians and French from the 7th Jägerbattalion.[5]

Other units had their first taste of fraternisation on Christmas Day, although this was sometimes not so straightforward in execution. George Ashurst, an NCO with the 2nd Battalion, East Lancashire Regiment, described how the initial German appeal for friendship in his section of the line ended up with the messenger in question being taken prisoner:

> About 10 o'clock, something like that in the morning, or half-past, a Jerry's walking across and he has a stick with a white flag on it and he's walking across towards our lines. Course, when he gets halfway he stops, which he has to do, you know, waiting for somebody to bring him in. So we sent a fellow out from our lot [who] went to him, met him, brought him in. Well, he's a prisoner of war! When he gets in our lines he's immediately a prisoner of war. We've got to keep him as a prisoner of war and we have to tell him so, because he's not been blindfolded. That fellow who went out for him should have blindfolded him, and *then* brought him in. But he didn't, so our officers had to tell him he was a prisoner of war … Anyhow, the message said like 'Could we have an armistice of two hours, from 11 o'clock till 1', that's what the message was. And our people agreed, they sent a messenger back. It came 11 o'clock of course and we'd been standing up on the firing parapet, and nobody was shooting and Jerry was doing same, so one or two fellows jumped out on top and another or two stopped in the trench with their rifles ready … but as these two fellows got up, others followed and there were scores of us on top.[6]

One of the most immediate and popular excuses for arranging a ceasefire appears to have been the collection and burial of the dead lying out in No Man's Land, as Lieutenant Menke of the 15th (2nd Westphalian) Infantry

1. Pope Benedict XV (1854–1922)

2. Field Marshal Sir John French (1852–1925), commander of the British Expeditionary Force.

3. General Sir Horace Smith-Dorrien (1858–1930), commander of the British II Corps and, from 26 December 1914, Second Army.

4. General Sir Douglas Haig (1861–1928), commander of the British I Corps and, from 26 December 1914, First Army.

5. Rupprecht, Crown Prince of Bavaria (1869–1955), commander of the German Sixth Army.

6. German soldiers singing carols in their trench, alongside a lit Christmas tree.

7. A typical German Christmas card from 1914.

8. This British Christmas card from 1914 stresses the partnership of the Allied nations.

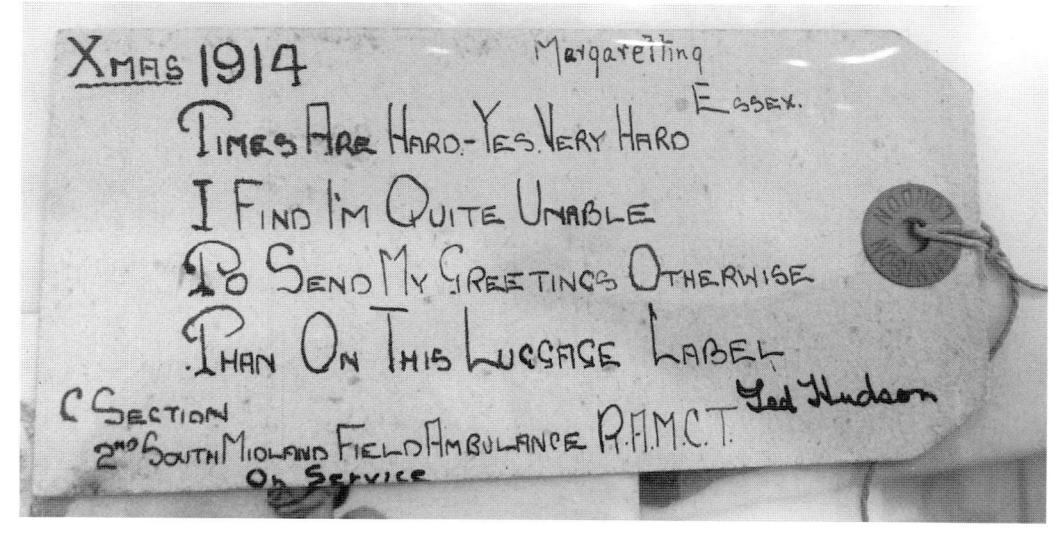

9. Soldiers at the front would use whatever means they could to get a message home to their loved ones. This soldier chose to send home an annotated luggage label as a novel souvenir.

11. *The Illustrated London News* of 9 January 1915.

12. An internal illustration from the same journal gives an artist's depiction of the fraternisation.

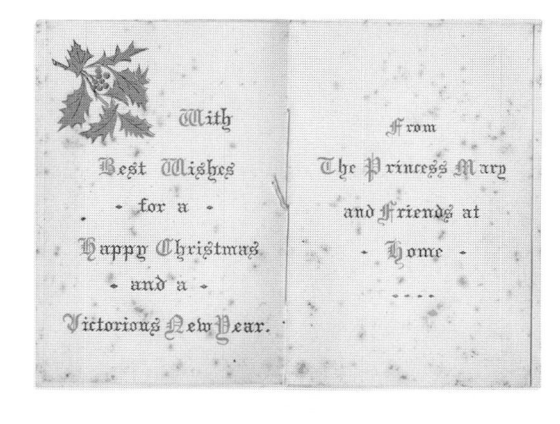

10. Around 400,000 gift boxes such as this were distributed to the British troops at Christmas 1914 on behalf of Princess Mary.

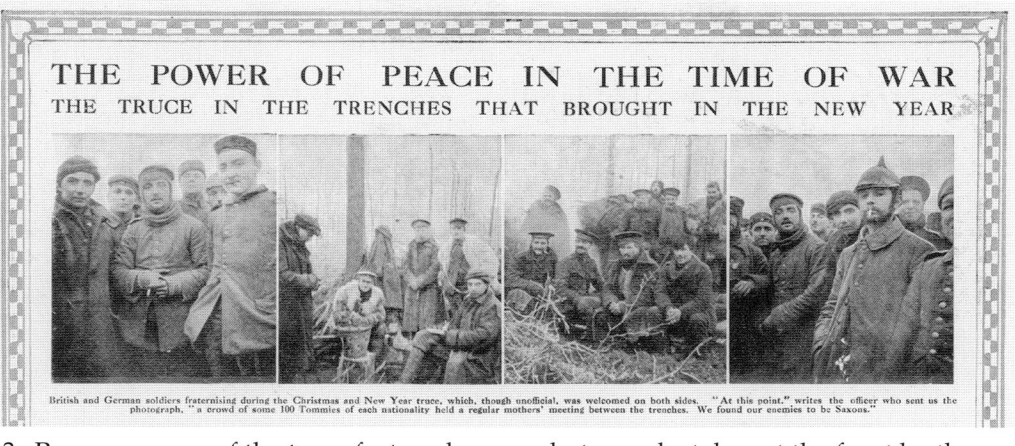

THE POWER OF PEACE IN THE TIME OF WAR
THE TRUCE IN THE TRENCHES THAT BROUGHT IN THE NEW YEAR

British and German soldiers fraternising during the Christmas and New Year truce, which, though unofficial, was welcomed on both sides. "At this point," writes the officer who sent us the photograph, "a crowd of some 100 Tommies of each nationality held a regular mothers' meeting between the trenches. We found our enemies to be Saxons."

13. Press coverage of the truce featured many photographs taken at the front by the participants.

The Daily Mirror

AN HISTORIC GROUP: BRITISH AND GERMAN SOLDIERS PHOTOGRAPHED TOGETHER.

14. *The Daily Mirror* of 8 January 1915.

15. Many commemorative coins were struck to mark the First World War centenary in 2014, including this Christmas Truce example. It is unfortunately based upon an original photograph incorrectly attributed to the infamous football match!

16. This modern memorial to the truce, 'All Together Now' by Andy Edwards, is located in the grounds of St Luke's Church, Liverpool.

Regiment would suggest. The British attacks a week or so before Christmas had resulted in a significant number of soldiers remaining missing, their bodies lying scattered on the rough ground between the trenches, still to be identified and recovered.

> Early morning on 25 December our guard became aware of the English standing on their ramparts and waving a white flag. One of our officers climbed out of the trench and waited until two English officers approached. In a delightful gibberish they agreed on a local ceasefire that was agreed to last from 11am to 1pm in order to bury the many English dead. At 11am English work squads arrived in order to put the corpses into a large ditch they had dug out at the periphery of the field. Soon our men joined and helped them. When they had finished with their work, towards 1pm, an English officer approached our battalion aide asking whether we had a clergyman among our lot. While our battalion didn't include a priest, we did have a student of theology who served with us and he was called to assist. A delegation of English assembled at one side of the mass grave and the German delegation on the other. We recited together an English prayer, followed by the Lord's Prayer in both languages and then had a few moments' silence. At the end, officers of both sides, as such enemies, shook each other's hands. With that, this curious war ceremony came to an end.[7]

Requests to hold ceasefires in order to collect and bury the dead were similarly instigated by the Germans. Even those units and individuals reluctant to commit to fraternisation could justify the need to establish a temporary armistice for such a humane purpose. Some would have been mindful of the orders received from higher up their chains of command about the dangers of fraternising with the enemy, yet a mutual arrangement to clear No Man's Land could surely be regarded as a legitimate excuse to halt the war for an agreed period. Sergeant Arthur Self of the 2nd Battalion, West Yorkshire Regiment, was based in the Neuve Chapelle sector:

> Just after breakfast in the front line a white flag appeared in the German trench. A bit later we responded and all firing ceased. A German officer left his trench and met one of ours in the centre of No Man's Land. Speaking English, he offered an armistice so that an unarmed party (stretcher bearers) could bury our dead lying behind the German front line. A sergeant and six men wearing red cross armlets crossed over and carried out this task, which took about two hours. During this period I was able to bury the Lance Sergeant in a grave about four yards behind our front line. This was in full view of the German front line – no mourners, no chaplain, just myself – in a shallow grave and a small wooden cross. The task finished, I jumped down into the trench thankful that Fritz had kept faith to the truce. Later on, the burial party returned to our lines. There were no planes overhead, no observation balloons, no bombs, no rifle fire, therefore no snipers, just an occasional lark overhead. Just watching … and watching, it was so quiet, it was uncanny, two forces facing each other in the muddy trenches, sentries posted at each periscope, which were put up without being shot at. The truce ended at 10pm with a burst from a Maxim.[8]

In some cases, soldiers from both sides ended up working together to collect and bury the fallen, as Eduard Tölke of the 17th Bavarian Infantry Regiment observed. Although wariness remained as the soldiers carefully kept their distance from the opposite trenches, it was only natural for one soldier to seek to assist another while carrying out such a benevolent and humane task.

> In actual fact it had only been agreed that each side would lay their own dead soldiers to rest, but soon rather strange things were happening in No Man's Land between the two front lines. Our people began helping the enemy to bury their dead. You could see lit trees everywhere and it was a very festive scene, all the more so due to zero wind and glorified by the white frost.[9]

Further joint burial services were held, with one of the largest being arranged near Fleurbaix, just south-west of Armentières, to bury about a hundred dead of the Gordon Highlanders, Scots Guards and the 15th (Westphalian) Infantry Regiment. 2nd Lieutenant Spence Sanders of the 1/6th Battalion, Gordon Highlanders, recalled how the day so far was turning out to be 'a jolly queer Christmas':

> It was a hard frost last night so we had a miserable cold time in our dug-out. The casualties yesterday were bad. Two men killed – one in 'D' Company and one in 'F'; several wounded, one in 'E' badly in the shoulder. This morning the Colonel came down and the Padre – the latter was going to bury the 'F' Company man. While talking to them, an order came along not to shoot. Very shortly we found the Germans were getting out of the trenches and our men were doing the same. They walked across and met and talked to each other. I went over and talked to some. A tremendous lot of dead were lying about. Very soon an order came to return to the trenches but then another came to send our parties to bury the dead. The Germans did the same and we all mixed up and chatted. The dead were a horrible sight – nearly all Borderers left after the charge. The German

dead had been there much longer I believe and were quite rotten. The Germans were a nice lot, though – as fed up as we are. There is to be no firing for an hour after the burying and unofficially I believe it is agreed that there will be none either today or tomorrow. I only hope there won't be – I have seen enough horrors for one day.[10]

There were many other smaller burial ceremonies. A witness to one of these was Henry Williamson, who recalled how discussions between soldiers from the two opposite sides drifted inevitably towards the subject that brought them together in the first place – the war.

> The Germans started burying their dead which had frozen hard, and we picked up ours and we buried them and little crosses of ration-box wood were nailed together, quite small ones, and indelible pencil. They were putting on the Germans *'Fur Vaterland und Freiheit'* – 'For Fatherland and Freedom' – and I said to a German, 'Excuse me, but how can you be fighting for freedom? You started the war, and we are fighting for freedom.' And he said, 'Excuse me, English *kamerad*, but we are fighting for freedom for our country and I say also put "Here rests in God an unknown hero in God". Oh yes, God is on our side.' But I said, 'He is on our side.' And that was a tremendous shock, I began to think that these chaps who like ourselves, whom we liked and who felt about the war as we did, and who said, 'It will be over soon because we shall win the war in Russia,' and we said, 'No, the Russian steamroller is going to win the war in Russia.' 'Well, English comrade, do not let us quarrel on Christmas Day.'[11]

The regimental history of the 17th Bavarian Infantry Regiment draws particular attention to the interactions of the fraternising soldiers. The situation could become rather ridiculous. One minute they were sharing the burden of burying their dead with all the emotions attached to such a grim task; the next, they were chatting about their lives back home, playing games and exchanging jokes:

> [We] are honouring a dead Englishman, toss a handful of earth onto the corpse and offer up the Lord's Prayer to accompany him to the world beyond. North of the Ploegsteert Woods some German and English soldiers together bury two French and it is the German officer who says the prayers in this instance. He then asks the English sergeant to cut his hair. There he is, kneeling in No Man's Land and fully trusting, while having his hair cut with a knife and scissors dangerously wielded by his enemy around his neck.[12]

As locally arranged burial parties and ceasefires spread across Flanders, so too did the opportunity for soldiers of both sides to meet directly with one another. Aware of the unique circumstances of the truce, occurring on Christmas Day itself – which after all was traditionally the time to exchange gifts with one another and share food and drink – soldiers would come together to do exactly those things, mirroring as far as they could their traditional Christmas back home. This was all accompanied by proper conversation, not just shouted exchanges as regularly practised by the trench inhabitants but in some cases very detailed discussions, as remembered by Colin Wilson of the 1st Battalion, Grenadier Guards:

> Our officers allowed a limited number of us to go into No Man's Land and there we were, chatting away, and we finished up by singing carols and talking in all sorts of things

about the war and other things. Well I met a very perfect English-speaking German soldier who told me he'd lived practically all his previous life in England. He looked upon England as his home where he had many friends. But he'd made a mistake; he'd visited his dying father in Germany just before the war started 1914 and he wasn't allowed to return to England. The war was about to begin and so he was sent into the German Army. He said, 'How I would have loved to have been interned in Alexandra Palace for the war, it would have been much better than this!'[13]

Leslie Walkinton similarly found his interaction with the Germans to be both an exciting and remarkable experience:

We met one another and had a chat halfway between the two lines of trenches and exchanged buttons, cigars and cigarettes. It was really funny to see the hated antagonists standing in groups laughing and talking and shaking hands. I got a German button and two cigars and a cigarette. One or two of them actually came from London and said they hoped to return after the war. Of course we didn't talk about who was going to win or anything touchy like that. They were 102nd Saxons and were decent chaps apparently. Several had got Iron Crosses, we asked one chap what he had done to win it and he didn't seem to know. They had just heard the Germans had taken Buckingham Palace! Their clothes were not very good and they seemed a bit jealous of our goatskin coats. They had got half-wellington boots and grey uniforms and wore little round hats without peaks. Of course none of us carried rifles. It was a beautiful day and the ground was white with frost. Some of them were trying to arrange a football match but it didn't come off. Talk about peace and goodwill, I never saw a friendlier sight. We tried to explain to each other that we bore no malice. One of their officers took a photo of a group of intermingled troops, they were not so strong looking as English fellows and some were much smaller than even I. I feel much more confident about a bayonet charge now, although I believe they usually run away before our fellows get within 50 yards.[14]

Just as the British troops were fascinated to see German troops up close, the novelty of meeting with the foe was not lost on the Germans. They recognised too that the opportunity was a mutual exercise in intelligence-gathering. The need to seek useful information about the enemy entrenched opposite was ingrained into the mind of every front-line soldier, and it is therefore unsurprising that, given their sudden proximity and openness, men of both sides often kept this in mind throughout any meetings. Some would in fact use the gathering of intelligence as an excuse to justify such friendly chats in the first place, as Fridolin Solleder of the 16th Reserve Infantry Regiment recalled:

> We could never have gathered such information (in detail) from even our most skilled patrols and much related bloodshed. This is the fruit of German–English brotherhood over the Christmas days. The English trenches were laid out in three rows behind each other, the forward-leaning barbed wire was fortified by a square or rectangular outpost. The English infantry consisted of young men, down to 15 years of age and men of over 40. Their training had lasted between three and six months, but they also had some experienced squads. They were all equipped beautifully, wore lace-up boots, nearly all of them wore fur jackets of sheepskin, and many even wore fur coats. They made a good impression on the Germans. They told us about disagreements and even fist-fights between the French and the English.

Compared to the tinned meat which they gave our men, our food from the field kitchen is too thin and too greasy and gives cause for complaint. They too gifted us newspapers, postcards and pipes. Even now some of our comrades keep pictures of English soldiers, along with the Christmas wishes written on them in No Man's Land, as dear memorabilia of the 1914 Christmas. Max Herold of the 8th Company still owns three of them and on one of them is written, 'Wishing you a very happy Christmas and to a speedy ending of the war. I. A. Praer, 15 Devonshire.' It was a sacred time, these days from 22 to 29 December, and our regiments did not suffer any dead or injured, because Tommy kept entirely quiet.[15]

Some German soldiers spoke English very well, having been reservists who had spent time in Britain in the years before the outbreak of war. Many had found employment as waiters in hotels or restaurants, as well as barber shops, particularly in London. The shared understanding through language helped to emphasise the common experience of the soldier in the trenches as Rupert Frey, also of the 16th Reserve Infantry Regiment, recognised:

It was miraculous! These were Englishmen, English soldiers of whose existence we only knew based on their iron-wrapped missives, and now, here we were face-to-face. The two of us who had been lying opposite each other gun in hand were now waving to each other, exchanging gifts as if we had been friends, brothers even! Well, indeed, isn't that precisely what we were! At that moment we were friends, no longer German and English – we were human beings![16]

Among those fraternising was Graham Williams, who was particularly keen to acquire some souvenirs of what was already being seen by the participants as a remarkable event in the course of the war. However, the limited personal possessions belonging to troops while on active service meant that there were not too many options when it came to finding suitable items to exchange with their new-found comrades.

> We, the Territorials, wore metal shoulder titles; ours said 'T 5 City of London' which meant 'Territorial 5th Battalion City of London Regiment'. We always resented these shoulders titles because our real name was the London Rifle Brigade; we objected to being called the 5th London. Anyway, I thought it was a good opportunity to get rid of one of these, so I swapped it with a German for his leather equipment belt, an ordinary leather belt but with a brass buckle with '*Gott Mit Uns*' on it ... I got this buckle and this belt and [got] talking to all these Germans and then our officer came along just then and wanted me to interpret for him, because he was going to meet a German officer to arrange about burying a lot of dead cows which were between the trenches and beginning to smell a bit. There were also a few corpses of British troops from an attack we'd made about a few days earlier. So this was all fixed up, I translated for him to this German officer and that was all arranged and they fixed up working parties of Germans and British, all digging pits and hauling these cows into them and so forth.
>
> After a bit I was talking to some other Germans, and I was walking along and a chap came up to me, he actually greeted me with the words, 'Whatcha, cock, how's London?' I said, 'Good Lord, you speak English?' 'Well,' he said, 'I *am* English'. 'No,' I said, 'you speak like a Londoner.' He said, 'Well I *am* a Londoner.' I said, 'Well what in hell are you doing in the German Army?' He said, 'Well I'm a German. I'm a German Londoner.' And apparently he'd been born in

Germany but he'd gone to England immediately afterwards with his parents and they had a small business in the east end of London somewhere and he'd been brought up in England and gone to school in England and everything. But when he became due for his military service, as by German law he was still a German national – well he was by our law because he'd never been naturalised – he was called up to go to Germany to do his national service. He finished that, they did three years of it at that time, and after that he came back to London and joined his parents and he got a job as a porter at Victoria station. He told me all this. Anyway, he spoke absolute cockney, it was an extraordinary thing really.[17]

*

Such local truces combined across Flanders to consolidate the larger Christmas Truce which held firm over more than two-thirds of the British line, but in some areas there was still no ceasefire, no fraternisation, nor any friendly communication at all. Due to the variable terrain, the rudimentary quality of communications and the self-contained operational nature of infantry battalions, it was entirely possible not to be aware of what was going on in other areas, even neighbouring sectors. Some units would only learn of the Christmas Truce some days or weeks after the event. In addition, many simply could not entertain the idea of fraternisation. For them, it seems the conditions were simply not right – perhaps there was no urgent need to recover dead from No Man's Land, maybe their trenches did not require any critical repair, or possibly they simply remained distrustful of their enemy. This latter motive appears to have been the reason that the German Lieutenant Hans Keller, of the 13th Infantry Regiment, refused to support a truce. He wrote the following letter on

27 December which was published in his local newspaper back home in the town of Goch, located close to the German border with the Netherlands:

> We spent Christmas in the trenches and currently there is no point even dreaming about being replaced, as the past days have been marked by hard work, blood and fighting. An English attack, causing heavy injuries, collapsed. But there is no knowing whether it won't be repeated in the next few days. Therefore, all of us have to be on high alert. When our trees stood lit atop the parapet and our renderings of *Stille Nacht, Heilige Nacht*' filtered through the ranks, we didn't let down our guard and kept hundreds of guns and shining bayonets directed against the enemy trenches located only some 50 to 100 metres away. Our hatred is too overpowering for it to leave room for melancholic thoughts over Christmas. If they had indeed attacked they certainly wouldn't have found us lost in dreams and wishful thinking. Once we are replaced, I will immediately distribute the gifts among the men. They will show their gratitude to those benevolent donors by continuing to pledge commitment to war and risking their life, heart and soul.[18]

Much first-hand testimony from British and French participants suggests that Saxons were invariably keener to offer the olive branch of friendship than Prussians. Perhaps the ancestral heritage which the Saxons believed that they shared with the English might have encouraged feelings of fraternity. Also, certain battalions and regiments were always less likely to consider fraternisation than others, based on their long-standing reputations and traditions.

Evidence certainly exists to indicate that in some cases peaceful offers from one side were swiftly rejected by the other, or at the very least treated with a degree of suspicion. The war diary of the German 17th Reserve Infantry Regiment illustrates how units remained on constant alert despite the ceasefire, since there was always the opportunity for the enemy to take advantage of the situation and strike at an opportune moment. Such caution is regularly expressed in both private and official accounts of the Christmas Truce – a quite understandable concern when dealing with those who had been considered, up until that moment, as a sworn enemy:

> Very festive and atmospheric Christmas celebrations took place, but any kind of fraternising with the enemy was strictly prohibited, while at the same time all useless shooting was also forbidden. [We] emphatically alerted all companies that the enemy remained fully convinced that during Christmas time an attack by them would be successful. They … firmly believe that we [the Germans] go to great length celebrating this holy day regardless of it being war and that our troops would therefore not be vigilant. Let us therefore first complete what we need to do and then go on to celebrate a joyful Christmas in Comines.[19]

Such distrust worked both ways. The war diary for the 1st Battalion, Bedfordshire Regiment, indicates that their contribution to the Christmas Truce consisted of only slightly reducing their usual aggression over the Christmas period. A more direct appeal for peace came from the Germans on Boxing Day, but the Bedfordshires were not to be enticed into any kind of friendliness:

> Another quiet day. A little shelling by both sides. Some Germans came forward unarmed, apparently with a view to friendly intercourse. A few shots fired in their direction as a hint to withdraw.[20]

For these units, the war therefore continued as normal. Indeed, even within sectors where the Christmas Truce was holding strong, some dissenting voices could still be heard who disagreed with the entire notion of calling a temporary halt to the fighting. How could the war be fought and won if each nation's soldiery were so ready to show friendship and understanding towards their enemy? Differences of opinion certainly existed, even within particular units. While the 2nd Battalion, Northamptonshire Regiment, had arranged for a ceasefire with the Germans opposite them to last for the entirety of Christmas Day, it seems that not all those in the opposing trenches were firmly convinced by the olive branch of friendship. Despite the ceasefire being maintained successfully over the agreed period, certain Germans sent over a note to the British, which read as follows:

> Gentlemen, you asked us yesterday to temporarily suspend hostilities and to become friends during Christmas. Such a proposal in the past would have been accepted with pleasure but at the present time when we have clearly recognised England's real character, we refuse to make such an agreement. Although we do not doubt that you are men of honour, yes, every feeling of ours revolts against any friendly intercourse towards the subject of a nation which for years has, in an underhand way, sought the friendship of all other nations, that with their help they might annihilate us; a nation also which, while professing Christianity, is not ashamed to use dum-dum bullets; and whose greatest pleasure would be to see the political disappearance and social eclipse of Germany.
>
> Gentlemen you are not, it is true, the responsible leaders of British politics and so you are not directly responsible for their baseness, but all the same you are Englishmen

whose annihilation we consider to be our most sacred duty. We therefore request you to take such action that will prevent your mercenaries, whom you call 'soldiers', from approaching our trenches in future.
  (Signed) Lieutenant of Landwehr.[21]

In some areas, Christmas Day still saw casualties sustained by both sides, despite ceasefires ostensibly being maintained. The 16th Bavarian Reserve Infantry Regiment suffered one such example, albeit due to an unfortunate mistake.

> In most companies the Christmas celebrations which took place were very spiritual and atmospheric. A sad incident occurred when reservist Eggel got killed by sheer accident (i.e. no shooting by the enemy) when he was cleaning his rifle and it unfortunately went off. This ruptured the peace.[22]

In a more blatant disregard of the ceasefire arrangements, two men from the 2nd Battalion, Monmouthshire Regiment, were both shot in the back while returning from fraternising with the Germans. A corporal from the 5th Battalion, Scottish Rifles, was similarly shot after a British soldier fired his rifle by mistake and the Germans swiftly retaliated in kind. But these incidents were all followed by a German apology. It seems more than possible that these soldiers had approached too near to the enemy's trenches, and then when realising their mistake and attempting to flee were treated as escaping prisoners. Further casualties were also sustained due to the hasty actions of neighbouring troops who, not involved in any such arrangement themselves, spotted intruders in No Man's Land and opened fire on them.

Once any agreed period of ceasefire was finished, certain areas would experience casualties almost immediately. The war diary of the 2nd Battalion, Devonshire Regiment, serves as a cold example of how both peace and war could exist on the same day, in this case in the Neuve Chapelle sector:

> 25 December: Informal armistice during daylight. Germans got out of their trenches and came towards our lines. Our men met them and they wished each other a Merry Christmas, shook hands, exchanged smokes, etc. About 7.30pm sniping began again. We had one man killed and one wounded. Hard frost.[23]

For those sectors which did not enjoy any involvement in the Christmas Truce, the Christmas period was largely business as usual, with corresponding casualties. The Commonwealth War Graves Commission records ninety-one British soldiers as having been killed on Christmas Day 1914 and, although German statistics are more difficult to establish, their casualties are most likely to have been more than comparable.

*

For many of the infantry units involved in the Christmas Truce, the day would continue to be filled with further opportunities for fraternisation which led to several occasions when good humour was enjoyed by both sides. Captain Sir Edward Hulse of the 2nd Battalion, Scots Guards, recalled one of the most famous such incidents:

> Just after we had finished *Auld Lang Syne* an old hare started up, and seeing so many of us about in an unwonted spot, did not know which way to go. I gave one loud 'View Holloa', and one and all, British and Germans, rushed about giving chase, slipping up on the frozen plough, falling about, and after a hot two minutes we killed in the open, a German

and one of our fellows falling together heavily upon the completely baffled hare. Shortly afterwards we saw four more hares, and killed one again; both were good heavy weight and had evidently been out between the two rows of trenches for the last two months, well-fed on the cabbage patches, etc., many of which are untouched on the no-man's land. The enemy kept one and we kept the other.[24]

In the trenches held by Scottish units, the sound of bagpipes could be heard drifting across No Man's Land while German bands struck up their own renditions of popular songs. One private of the 3rd Battalion Rifle Brigade, Jack Reagan, had his hair cut by a Saxon barber who by a remarkable coincidence already knew him from High Holborn in London. Captain Josef Sewald from the 17th Bavarian Reserve Regiment recalled this and other bizarre situations:

> Just try and imagine ... We are in the midst of a war and there is this barber and he totally couldn't have given a damn, but there he was and in exchange for a few cigarettes he cut the hair of a soldier, not giving a jot whence his client came, whether it was from this side or the other. And it went even further. Many of the men, enemies moments before, began cutting each other's hair which, believe me, was an even odder sight, as they of course didn't have a stool like Reagan. So what happened was that one kneeled in front of the other, dozens of them followed suit, all mixed together, young German and Englishmen who burst out laughing with their faces covered in shaving cream and then merrily stomping dead the lice that lay hidden in the chopped-off hair bundles. One couldn't detect even the slightest sign of hostile feelings between any of them! I never thought this could happen.[25]

Tales of an alleged football match between the British and Germans have now become the stuff of legend. Perhaps it was natural for the men of both sides to want to participate in a game of the most popular sport enjoyed by the working classes. It was also one of the most simple sports to arrange, requiring only a ball (or a substitute object to withstand kicking) and rough goal posts. However, despite the myth of a well-organised game between England and Germany being enjoyed in No Man's Land, the surviving evidence suggests that this did not occur. Instead, it seems to have been the case that while a number of games of football *did* happen during the Christmas Truce, these were rough 'kickabouts' rather than properly organised and refereed matches.

One of the best accounts of football during the Christmas Truce is provided by Ernie Williams, an inexperienced 19-year-old volunteer soldier with the 6th Battalion, Cheshire Regiment. Having embarked for the front in October, he had only been on active service for a few weeks when Christmas arrived. On 25 December his unit were in the trenches near Messines, looking forward to being relieved the following day.

> When early morning came it was rather misty and, looking over the top of the trench, you could see in No Man's Land four figures, four or five, a little group. And then from right and left there was a swarm out of the line to join with them … So we got a great big mass of soldiers there. Mind you, the officers when we started swarming over the trench tried to push us back, some of them [shouting] 'Get back you bloody fools,' and all that sort of thing, but we didn't take any notice. The officers were a separate entity to us, they didn't fraternise with us. They tried to stop us when we were going over, definitely. I can see now one officer was

shaking his hands, 'You bloody fools, get back, you don't know what you're doing.' Well, he thought it was a trap, like I thought.

Soon it was a mass of soldiery in No Man's Land, exchanging cigarettes, goodies from Christmas parcels and what have you. The people in front of us were Bavarians, some of them had great big beards. I was only 19, I was scared to death. We shared fags, goodies with the Germans. And then from somewhere, somehow, this football appeared. It appeared from somewhere, I didn't know where, but it came from their side – it wasn't from our side where the ball came. It was a proper football and they kicked it about. They made goals and one fellow went in goal and then it was just a general kickabout. I should think there would be at least about a couple of hundred [taking part]. I had a go at it. I was pretty good then, at 19. It was a proper football but we didn't form a team, it wasn't a team game in any sense of the word, it was like how I learned my football in Hill Gate streets ... you know, it was a kickabout, everybody was having a go. There was no score, no tally at all. It was simply a melee – nothing like the soccer you see on television. In fact the boots you wore were a menace – those great big boots you had on – in those days the balls were made of leather and they soon got very soggy. They took their coats off, some of them did, and put them down as goal posts. Well it went on for about, as far as I was concerned it wasn't more than an hour, but some of them were there for about three or four hours.

Everybody seemed to be enjoying themselves. There was no sort of ill-will between us. There were some of them that could speak English, the Germans. I don't think many of our side could speak German. There was no referee, you didn't need a referee for that sort of a game, it was like playing as a kid in the streets, kicking the ball about in the street and the referee being the policeman and chasing you off! As far as I was concerned it didn't last a long time because, I'll be quite frank, I didn't trust them.[26]

While the Christmas Truce fraternisation is so often described in terms of mutual friendship and trust, Ernie's recollections are particularly interesting for their honest perspective. As a nervous, inexperienced young soldier, he suddenly found himself unexpectedly mixing with the enemy whom he'd been trained to fight. It was a bizarre situation and the exchange of gifts such as cigarettes caused him great concern, not only because he worried about the Germans poisoning him, but due to his own inexperience as a smoker!

> Actually I was a bit scared. I'll admit that, I was really scared. Because in my bringing up you see, Sunday school and one thing or another, I'd always been told that you didn't smoke. If you smoked before you were 21 you'd stunt your growth, they used to tell the children that. So I'd made up my mind I wasn't going to smoke until I was 21. And I kept those cigarettes [presented by the Germans] for quite a time. I never smoked them because I was a bit innocent and thought, 'Oh, they might be doing something wrong,' you know. I didn't trust them because there had been so many atrocities, you see, building up to it ... so I got back to the line as soon as I could. I thought there was something wrong with the cigarettes, I didn't smoke them. I thought it could be [a trick] because there'd been a lot of atrocities that they were guilty about, they hadn't 'played the game' as it were properly, they'd ill-treated women and all sorts of things.[27]

However, not all troops were so suspicious. Johannes Niemann of the 133rd (9th Royal Saxon) Infantry Regiment found the whole experience of meeting with the enemy hugely entertaining. His particular sector of trench was opposite that manned by a Scottish regiment.

> One of our fellow Landseer soon found out, much to his great amusement, that the Scots don't wear underpants under their skirt, leaving their bare bottoms clearly visible for everyone to see the minute the skirt starts fluttering even a tiny bit. His report greatly entertained us and while at first we could hardly believe it to be true we were soon to be convinced otherwise. The scenes we witnessed were truly comical. The rabbits in the fields were hopping mad. Their Eldorado had, of course, come alive with human beings and what with Tommy and Fritz chasing them. Suddenly a Scotsman brought along a football and an honest-to-God game ensued with our caps serving as goal posts … Quite a few centre passes missed their target as, given the field – a frozen sea of ruts and troughs – a regular game simply wasn't possible. But all the players and all the spectators were united in sportsmanship. One of us had a camera. The football players quickly formed an orderly group, lined up properly, football in the middle … We kept to the rules, though the game only lasted for one hour and we didn't have a referee. Fritz won with the score 3–2. We Germans whistled and hooted every time a gust of wind lifted the skirts of the Scots and revealed the fact that they wore no underwear. After the hour was over, our officer ordered us to end the game. We returned to our trenches and this too put an end to the period of fraternisation.[28]

Other participants were less enamoured of the extent of fraternisation that was developing on Christmas Day. A temporary truce to bury the dead was one thing, but football matches were another entirely. So felt Gustav Riebensahm of the 15th (2nd Westphalian) Infantry Regiment:

The English are especially grateful for the ceasefire as finally they are able to play football. But this whole business is beginning to be ludicrous and needs to stop. I agree with the 55th [another unit in the same brigade] that tonight this is coming to an end.[29]

Sport is also briefly mentioned by George Ashurst, of the 2nd Battalion, East Lancashire Regiment, who suggested that the inclination to play football might have been directly linked to the sudden opportunity to be out in the open of No Man's Land, and the desire to make the most of the unexpected freedom and space.

> Oh, it was grand. You could stretch your legs and run about on the hard surface ... and we tied a sandbag up, an empty sandbag, we tied it up with itself in string and kicked it about on top. Just to keep warm, of course. And Jerry, he was sliding on a pond, we could tell he was sliding on an ice pond the way he started off, you know, and went so gently across to the other end and another followed him. We could tell they were sliding on a pond, just behind the lines.
> We did not intermingle. Only, partway through this armistice we were all playing football and all on top, Jerry was all on top, and some Jerries came to their wire with a newspaper and they were waving it, you know ... a corporal in our company went for it, a bit lower down in our trench ... he got halfway and he stopped, I don't know whether he changed his mind or not, but the lads shouted, 'Go on, go on, get the paper!' So he did when they shouted to him like that. He went right to the wire and the Germans shook hands with him, wishing him Merry Christmas sort of thing, giving him their paper. And he came back just like a good soldier. Of course we couldn't read a word of it so it had to go to an officer, they got it. And that was the

armistice. And do you know, there were fellows walking about on top of our trench, *our* fellows, at 5 o'clock at tea time, and not a shot had been fired. And the armistice finished at 1 o'clock.[30]

In some areas, fraternisation only really began in the afternoon. This was perhaps linked to the shared need by both sides to undertake regular duties throughout the morning, or perhaps was even down to such a simple reason as observing the regular lunchtime of around midday. Some fraternisation commenced later in the day because the morning mist only rose in the early afternoon, allowing the opposite trenches to be observed more clearly for the first time. This was certainly the case in the part of the line held by the 2/39th Battalion, Royal Garhwal Rifles, located south of Neuve Chapelle. The Indian Corps had played an important role in the earlier December offensive, and many of their soldiers had already been withdrawn before Christmas began. But two battalions of the Garhwal Rifles remained in the line, suffering from severely waterlogged trenches. The German trenches further up were being pumped out, and the water was running down a natural ditch and ending up in the British 24th Infantry Brigade sector.

Captain Walther Stennes, although only 19 years of age, was a company commander in the 16th Westphalian Infantry Regiment. He attended military school in Germany since the age of 9 and had already gained the reputation of a veteran among his men. On Christmas Eve the unit had displayed their lit Christmas trees above the trenches, to the delight of the Indian troops opposite. Although India was, and remains, a largely non-Christian country, with Hinduism the most widespread faith, Christmas festivals were not uncommon in the larger towns and cities where most Christians resided. India's biggest annual celebration was, of course, Diwali – the festival of light – which shared with Christmas an emphasis upon lit decorations. The Indian troops would therefore have likely been just as excited and interested as their British or French counterparts to see the German trees lit up in the darkness, and once again this appears to have encouraged the first steps toward fraternisation.

> Suddenly the officer came marching in [and] said, 'Sir, I think the enemy doesn't shoot and some of my men are in the open, showing themselves, no shot is fired,' and so on. Actually the whole thing was absolutely spontaneous, not even an officer knew anything about it. But then I rushed out of the dugout, I saw some men of my company standing right open in the front and waving and saying, 'Merry Christmas'. And on the other side also some Indian standing up and waving and so on. Then the men hesitated to advance to the middle between the fronts, first hesitating then later on stepping freely forward and in the middle of the trenches, between the trenches in No Man's Land, they met, shook hands and so on and then began talking. Then more men came out and suddenly No Man's Land was covered with Indian and German soldiers and so on who shook hands and later on returned, fetched some small presents and so on, then they exchanged presents everywhere.
>
> I met some English officers and also Indian officers, we shook hands ... we also talked as much as we could, English and German, but anyhow we understood each other and very interesting was that people warned each other [about] the places where mines were and that nobody stepped on the mines. Of course everybody was unarmed, not even a knife. That was given out as a rule. But the sentries were still standing on duty, rifle ready, on

both sides. Then later on, even some men of my company stayed in the British trenches, they were fed there and had a drink and returned I think about 10 o'clock at night. So they stayed there the whole afternoon, they stayed with the English and Indian troops.

Of course now the High Command, I think on both sides, I don't know what happened on the English side ... nobody had any idea about this whole thing, it was absolutely spontaneous. Without any preparation, not even a front officer knew anything about it. Then the next day not a single shot was fired. Then they said, 'In case we have to shoot again, we will fire first in the air,' both sides. On the 25th no shot was fired, both sides absolutely silent. Sometimes you could see somebody peeping out of the trench on the other side, but no shot, nothing. On the second day the British started shooting again but very high as nobody was hit. But then we knew they were maybe going to be relieved ... and we stayed in the trenches. The following day we knew there was a new troop opposite and we had to be careful again. Then the war started again.[31]

A report by Captain William Kenny of the 1/39th Battalion, Garhwal Rifles describes the event from the British perspective:

At about 2.30pm, as far as I am aware, a Rifleman came and told me that many of the enemy were standing up on their parapet unarmed and shouting to us. I went to the 'Gap' and there saw about 40 or 50 of the enemy as described. One or two called to us in English to come out and speak to them. Then one German came about 10 yards out of his trench and put a box of cigars on the ground. Lieutenant Welchman was then with me and he gave orders for all sentries to remain on the lookout at their posts.

CHRISTMAS DAY IN THE BRITISH SECTOR

A British cavalry officer attached to 4th Cavalry Machine Guns, who was about 10 yards on my left, came out of the 'Gap' trench and went towards the enemy. I then noticed that others on my left from the 2/39th Garhwalis were out of their trench and moving towards the enemy's trenches. On the impulse of the moment I also went out and Lieutenant Welchman, Captain Pearse 4th Cavalry and some of the men came out too. About 12 or 15 Germans approached us and came up and shook hands with us and wished us the Compliments of the Season. One or two spoke English. I ordered them not to come nearer our line than halfway. I then asked permission to bury the dead that were lying there: this was accorded and our men buried on the spot one Jemir and four Riflemen of the 2/3rd and Jemir Kushal Takuli and Rifleman Thepru [of] F Company, 1/39th G. Their identity discs were searched for but not found. One dead man was lying right at the foot of the German parapet and three men of H Coy were permitted to go right up to the German trench there. One or two others of our men were given brandy and cigarettes right close to the German trench. Afterwards two German Subalterns came out and spoke to us. The men were all of the 16th Saxon Regiment. I asked them this (as I can talk a little German). They told me they were Saxons and not Prussians. I did not notice any other regiment amongst the men.[32]

Meanwhile, a senior officer from the neighbouring 1/39th Battalion, Garhwali Rifles spotted what was going on and sought to bring all fraternisation in this area of the front to a decisive halt:

I was told that Major Henderson was calling for me and I went back to him and he ordered me to bring all the men back into the trenches. Unfortunately I then noticed that a party of 4 or 5 Germans had come up to about 10 yards from our trench. I had previously given orders for no one to approach us closer than halfway. But these men could not have seen into our trenches as our barbed wire would have prevented them. They could not have located our Machine-Guns as these are dismantled and hidden during the day.[33]

The aftermath of the event was that two of the British officers involved faced a court martial for their actions in failing to stop the truce. Keen to acquit himself of having acted inappropriately, Captain Kenny attempted to justify his actions by stressing the importance of the intelligence that he had been able to gather as a direct result of the fraternisation. He was also quick to point out that it was a German who first came out halfway between the two trenches, while a British cavalry officer first greeted him and shook hands, instigating the beginning of the truce.

> I attach herewith a report on the German trenches, seen by our men and corroborated by two British Cavalry soldiers who also went up to the German parapet and helped to bury a dead Gurkha. Lieutenant Welchman noticed a printed postal address on a box of cigarettes, which a German soldier had been handing round – on it was printed the man's name, Army Corps (7th), Division (14th) and Regt (16th). Both the British Cavalry soldiers who helped to bury the dead Gurkha on the German parapet, state that at that time the Germans had completely evacuated their trenches, and were all outside and unarmed. Lieutenant Welchman and I estimate the numbers of the enemy we saw opposite the Gap and slightly to the left opposite the 2/39th as about 100.
> The German trenches in depth, width and general form resemble our own. The traverses seemed closer together, about 6 yards apart, but were not built right up to ground

level. The parapet is very thick at least 5'. Loopholes very strong and well made some with strong wooden sides tops and bottoms, the side walls of such loopholes being in some instances 3" thick. Other loopholes were made of galvanised iron, sides, tops and bottoms. There are 2 Machine-Guns in epaulments opposite the centre of the Gap, 6' separating the two epaulments. There is another Machine-Gun opposite a point 20 yds from the Right Corner of the Gap.

The men's shelters are like ours and cut out underneath the parapet. It appeared that there were considerably more men than loopholes. The trenches were clean and dry. There were no wire entanglements anywhere. There is a *chevaux-de-frize* [spiked obstacle] opposite the Left Centre of the Gap, but it is a good deal damaged. There were several ladders seen on the rear wall of the trench, but none on the front wall. But the ladders were movable and not fixed.[34]

Captain Kenny and Lieutenant Welchman's superiors were not convinced by their argument. The subsequent court martial resulted in a formal ticking off, and as a result the officers' leave was stopped ('a truly unnecessarily terrible penalty' according to Major Kenneth Henderson, the senior officer who had stopped the truce). Walther Stennes recalled a similar reaction to the situation from the German authorities, although in their case no particular culprits were blamed.

First they tried to court-martial us, but then instead it had to be confirmed who actually started the business. I think some people of my company tried first to wave and so on, and then get out, but it has never been established. They said, 'Oh well' ... I think at that time everybody wanted the war to come to an end, they would like to finish because they were all experienced troops on both sides and had enough of the war. But as nobody took any action later on, no court martial, nothing, then war went on as it had happened. We had not refused any order, that was out of the question, but the inner feeling was that we should make peace.[35]

In almost all accounts of the Christmas Truce from both sides, great care was usually taken to stop the enemy's soldiers from approaching too closely to the opposite trenches and thereby gain any useful intelligence. But despite this outward caution, there do appear to have been a few instances of troops visiting their opponents' trenches and sometimes even spending considerable time in them, although this generally resulted in the visitors being captured and held as prisoners of war for having seen too much. The 12th Infantry Brigade war diary records such an incident occurring in the St Yves sector on Christmas Day:

> Practically no sniping and no artillery fire all day. In left section, both sides sent parties out to bury dead between lines by daylight. At Le Touquet a German came into our lines to ask permission to bury dead. Having been allowed to see into our lines unarmed he could not be allowed to return.[36]

Some officers unquestionably saw the truce as an opportunity for some valuable intelligence-gathering. Military intelligence attached great importance to knowing as much about the opponent as possible, and such advice was regularly sent out to infantry units in order to emphasise the need for trench raids and other opportunities to investigate one's foe. As the following report sent by Lieutenant Colonel E. B. Cuthbertson, the officer commanding the 2nd Battalion, Monmouthshire Regiment, to the 12th Infantry Brigade on 22 December suggests, useful intelligence was a constant aspiration:

A sergeant (very trustworthy) states that in his opinion a different regiment is opposite them. He says the shooting is much better than before and says he calls the present enemy a good shooting regiment, the former a bad one. I have given instructions that they are to try to find out who is opposite them. They had a long shouted conversation which ended in vulgar abuse from the Germans when our men asked where the Kaiser was![37]

While in some cases the gathering of intelligence via fraternisation was apparently a deliberate intent, at other times one does wonder if such reports served as an opportune excuse to justify the unit having spent so much time in the company of the enemy. With regard to the Christmas Truce in particular, the following report provides an excellent detailed example of the kind of information which was being carefully collected during fraternisation. This list of intelligence was submitted to the 12th Infantry Brigade by Lieutenant Colonel Cuthbertson, and was compiled on Christmas Day itself:

1. Opposite No 4 Trench Germans were burying their dead. Men were sent out to see that no trenches were dug or any ruse employed. Some Germans had 104 in red cloth letters on shoulder straps. Buttons on their tunic had crowns. A belt was picked up from one of the dead which had 104 Regt 2nd Brigade 5th Corps.
2. Other men were wearing either RB or RP it is not certain which. They had different Nos 3, 4, 5, 6 on buttons and their shoulder straps. These men were wearing buttons with crowns.
3. Others again had 107 and 108 on shoulder straps the latter also having a crown.

4. There were also some seen wearing 181 on shoulder straps and 10 on buttons.
5. One officer was noticed wearing a cap similar to our Staff Officers cap, he was wearing spurs and had broad braid band on his cuff and 2 buttons.
6. Other officers were hard to distinguish from the men but were pointed out by a German soldier from Nottingham who gave their character such as very hard on the men, another was 'snotty' and another 'grumpy'; he also asked why our Officers do not come out. This German also spoke about pay and said German soldiers were getting 3/- a week on Service and their navies were paid 8/-. He also said they were paid on the 1st, 11th and 21st. He was sick of the war and stated that he had as many friends in England as in Germany.
7. Their NCOs carried torches on the buttons of their tunics and field glasses.
8. Signallers were seen with crossed flags.
9. Their uniforms were clean and their boots were very good.
10 They had plenty of tobacco and gave our men cigarettes and cigars and excellent socks. They offered them wine. It is interesting to note that one of our men being offered a glass of wine made the German sample it first.
11. They reported that the money was not much good to them as they stated the inhabitants had left behind them. [i.e. money was pointless due to there being little opportunity to spend it.]
12. The unoccupied trench in front of No 4 was full of dead bodies, nearly all shot through the head. The trench was merely head cover.
13. Several were wearing short sling coats like oilskins.
14. Our men reported that Germans were of all ages from 14 or 15 to 40 and 50.

15. A large majority wore glasses.
16. When they came out to bury their dead a party doubled out of the reserve trench.
17. Opposite No 4 they zigzagged through the entanglements.
18. Opposite No 2 they stepped over the barbed wire coming out, but had more difficulty in getting back.
19. At no time were the Germans allowed to approach our trenches and it was to prevent them coming too near that our men were sent out.
20. Capt Watkins reports that they were strongest opposite communication trench between 2 and 3 where we have no men.
21. It was noticed that while the Germans would talk English, on German being spoken they took cover like rabbits.
22. They sent out to apologise for shooting one of our men.[38]

*

Christmas Day had been a busy and eventful time, but as the daylight slowly faded, both sides gradually made their way back to their respective trenches. For some, this meant a final end to the Christmas Truce, with the end of the ceasefire usually signalled by the resumption of gunfire (albeit overhead, often in a pre-arranged fashion to signal the recommencement of the war). But in some areas, as we shall see, peaceful relations would resume after dawn, with the truce effectively still reigning for the next few days. Leslie Walkinton recalled that the ceasefire and fraternisation finished in his sector, occupied by the 1/16th Battalion, London Regiment (The Queen's Westminster Rifles), at dusk on Christmas Day:

When it was just beginning to get dark. I think as far as I remember we had arranged with one of our officers to demonstrate our wonderful discipline … when we thought it was about time that we'd better get back, we got him to come out and blow a whistle and say, 'Come on chaps'. And we turned as one man and walked back to our trenches.[39]

In some sectors, and especially among the soldiers located behind the lines in their billets, many still remained unaware of the scale of the Christmas Truce happening just a short distance away from where they were stationed. Some individuals, such as the German soldier Otto Hahn, had heard about the fraternisation that was going on but were still ignorant of how widespread it had become. On the evening of Christmas Day, Hahn wrote home to his wife Edith and wondered how she had celebrated the season in his absence.

I drank to your health with a glass of champagne and my thoughts were drifting, more intensely than ever, homewards. After all, it is our most cherished family celebration, and even in the open fields here far away, it is not possible to abandon tradition or disregard our belief in Christmas … It is 10.30pm in the evening, a deep calm surrounds me and I can only hear very far away, at a great distance from us, some faint rumblings of cannon fire. I am all alone in my cosy room at Warneton, which up to this night has served as our staff surgeon Scheiler's quarters. A clock is chiming away in a most agreeable way and all is quiet as if peace would reign supreme. It is quite unbelievable really; it is rather Christmassy. Around here, today, no shot has been fired, not during the evening either. It was a truce which was adhered to even more firmly *despite* everyone having expected the opposite. My machine-gun men say that it's likely there will be no shooting tomorrow either.[40]

By the end of the day, the relatively short section of the Western Front located in Flanders had seen multiple instances of ceasefires and fraternisation which in some cases would continue to last for some days and even weeks to come. The fact that the British held this part of the line meant that the Christmas Truce would always be associated chiefly with British and German participation, but there were certainly instances elsewhere along the line where French and Belgians were involved, as well as some limited fraternisation occurring on the Eastern Front. While these other examples of ceasefires are sometimes overlooked when discussing the Christmas Truce, there are clear reasons why they were not so marked or widespread as those in Flanders.

CHAPTER FIVE

The Christmas Truce Elsewhere

Rather than being one single organised event, the Christmas Truce could best be characterised as a spontaneous occurrence of smaller local arrangements which spread to encompass the Flanders region in particular, where the BEF was holding the line. Outside Flanders, the French offensives in Artois and Champagne were continuing, which provided little opportunity for either side to devote much attention to Christmas festivities. Yet away from Flanders there were certainly instances where ceasefires and fraternisation extended to include French and Belgian soldiers. The extent of this involvement in the larger Christmas Truce was notably different, and fraternisation with the Germans was rarely conducted in quite the same way as it played out in the British sector. For one thing, while there were definitely instances of camaraderie encouraged by the Christmas atmosphere which were embodied by singing and other festivities, there was very little meeting in large groups in No Man's Land.

Why was this? One of the most important aspects to consider is that although the British, French and other Allies were notionally fighting together against a common foe, each nation's army was arranged in quite distinct ways and liaison between them was organised at a higher level than that of the ordinary troops in the trenches. Each part of the front was clearly delineated from the other, and it is therefore no surprise that so many differences could be discerned between one sector and the next, even where those areas touched. Adjacent British sectors would usually operate quite independently anyway, with one experiencing fraternisation while its neighbour might not, and the added factor of different nationalities would mean even greater differences between one area and its neighbour. The war poet Robert Graves, a captain in the Royal Welsh Fusiliers, made reference to this relationship with the French when he observed that 'there's never any connexion between the two armies, unless a battle is on, and then we generally let each other down.'[1]

It may be helpful to distinguish between the different attitudes exhibited by each nation and the reasons why each was fighting, since these factors would greatly influence any feelings of benevolence which might have existed between them. German Artillery volunteer Rickner had arrived at the front in October 1914, and later reflected on how the typical German soldier tended to regard his enemies:

> Everybody thought of a war against France, nobody thought of England. And we were very disappointed and astonished when we learned ... that England had joined France and Russia. In any case, we thought our duty [was] to enter the army as soon as possible, everybody thought the war would be just like the war of 1870–71 against France, would last about four or five months.[2]

This attitude was widely shared by Germans. Why were the British involved in a war which didn't really concern them? This uncertainty and confusion perhaps encouraged any feelings of goodwill which might already have been felt by German soldiers towards the British, and which would be given the chance to bloom by the atmosphere and circumstances of Christmas 1914.

The relationship between Germany and France and Belgium, however, was clearly different. Each of these nations' respective roles was clear to all – the Germans were the invaders, while the French and Belgians were fighting to protect their homeland. To meet between the trenches in order to exchange compliments of the season would involve a complete change of mind-set for the French and Belgian soldiers. For them, the neutral strip of territory which was designated as No Man's Land for the British and Germans was in fact, unequivocally, their home soil. This was reinforced by the fact that French fighting was largely continuing throughout the Christmas period, unlike in Flanders where the British had effectively ceased campaigning towards the end of December.

However, despite such reasoning why friendly meetings between German, French or Belgian soldiers might be deemed unlikely, there is enough evidence from the months leading up to Christmas 1914 to suggest that fraternisation had been occurring on the Western Front on a fairly regular basis between these nations on multiple occasions. Indeed, it seems that the early months of the war saw a quite remarkable amount of 'live and let live' understanding developing between the invaders and those defending their homeland. The amount of direct fraternisation that was witnessed during November and December 1914 would in fact be much more obvious than that which occurred as part of the Christmas Truce.

The *Bergische Arbeiterstimme* newspaper printed some of the letters it had received from soldiers at the front, including the following example from an anonymous German NCO dated 14 January 1915. Referring to an incident that had occurred some weeks before, it shows how fraternisation between the Germans and French was by no means unknown:

> Dear Friends! I want to write to you about something which I myself have witnessed. It was a Sunday in November when our horn player called us out – our right-hand wing is situated

about 50 metres away from the enemy. The French appeared in droves outside their trenches, all standing atop the rampart and we showed them the cigarettes in our hands. They waved in response saying they would stop shooting and invited us to come across and they held their arms high. First, three of our regiment walked across and distributed cigarettes. It didn't take long for half of the company to appear assembled on the other side. I wasn't fully confident of the whole thing but a lieutenant then said to me, 'Sergeant, why don't you walk over there and inspect their positions.' That's what I did. I approached an officer, lit a cigarette and asked him if he also wanted to have a smoke. I gave him two cigarettes, actually these were my two last ones ... The officer then asked me if I too would like something and I responded, 'Yes, I wouldn't mind having a cognac,' whereupon he handed me the bottle and I helped myself to a good and proper swig. He then added that if we didn't shoot, they would do likewise; but if we started, then they would respond and shoot. He also added that every day they were hoping that there would be peace. I chatted to him for a whole hour. During the following three days there was no shooting between the two sides, but then we were replaced by another unit. Dear colleagues, you may well not believe it, but it is the honest truth.[3]

In a similar vein, the *Hallesche Volksblatt* newspaper published a letter penned by another anonymous German soldier, which may potentially be referring to the same ceasefire:

On the morning of the 28 November we, much to our surprise, saw how some of our [German] comrades located to the left of us ... emerged from their trenches while several French were walking towards our side; unarmed, they stretched out their hands to greet each other. Before you knew it, one of the French soldiers pulled out of his pocket a flask to then pass it to a German. Instantly more French soldiers consisting of cyclists and hussars happily waved to us with white drapes and caps from the other side. After having observed the whole spectacle quite closely, they finally dispatched one of their soldiers to approach our trenches with a friendship bottle in hand. Before too long a further group of twenty Germans and another group of roughly the same number of French were gathering around the same spot and shook each other's hands in a friendly greeting. It does seem incredible but is the truth. One might add that many, albeit not all, spoke enough German to be able to inform us that, so far and as far as their trenches were concerned, they had not shot a single bullet against us and that they were minded not to shoot if we also didn't shoot.[4]

Another example was provided in a letter dated 16 December from German soldier van Oyen of the 68th Infantry Regiment, which was printed in the Christmas edition of the Viersen local newspaper. Again, in this case it appears to have been the French soldiers who first offered the olive branch of friendship:

> All of a sudden, the French came out of their trenches, waved with their handkerchiefs and shouted something in French. 'Don't shoot'. They raised their arms above their heads, whereupon our front guards, calling across, assured them that they would not shoot and then the French approached. They, so they said, had had enough, there was no point in shooting each other dead; they were all married men. The French seemed a very amiable lot who offered our troops tobacco, chocolate etc. and saying that they intended to return and would bring some wine along. In the meantime, however, our officers have been apprised of the incident and that put a stop to things.

Nonetheless a few days later the French came across to us yet again, informing us that they had been ordered to shoot. Would we please withdraw to our trenches, keep our heads low and they would shoot above us. It turned out that the men in our position were well placed and had nothing to fear, as in the previous eight days not a single shot had been fired against them. This didn't last for too long either as the French officers must have got wind of it and one fine morning the shooting started all over again. Others had arrived to replace them in their positions.

And then the Frogs mentioned something else. Hadn't we realised that we had lost the war seeing as the Russians were only some 12 kilometres away from Berlin? That's how these red-pants have been taken for a ride. Our men then handed them some copies of our newspapers inviting them to read these, as some of them speak very good German. When they realised from what they had read what the actual situation really was, and recognising that they had suffered significant losses, they started railing against the English and claimed that they now wanted to join the Germans to fight England.[5]

Further exchanges of food and cigarettes were described by a German lieutenant from the 246th (Württemberg) Reserve Infantry Regiment, who similarly reported on fraternisation with the French:

> Suddenly, a beret appeared from the French trench some 40 metres away from us. *'Eh, camarad, pas tirer, brout brout, des cigarettes.'* ['Comrade, don't shoot, have some cigarettes'] Whereupon a German sniper immediately looked out from his trench. Shouting back, *'Bonjour, Monsieur'*, he flung his army bread over, and the Frenchman his cigarettes.[6]

As Christmas approached, the appetite for mutually arranged ceasefires appears to have grown among the French soldiers. The actor Paul Wegener, later to become famous for his roles in German expressionist cinema, served as a volunteer soldier in the Landwehr and recorded in his private diary how, as Christmas drew nearer, a temporary armistice understanding was established with the French troops opposite their position. But it was not to last for long.

> Towards lunchtime the shooting stopped altogether. Right next to us, an official ceasefire is being agreed on. The French have put out a white flag as a sign signalling that they intend to pause firing. On the other side we can observe people busily cooking away and once in a while we see dark silhouettes running back and forth against a backdrop of house ruins and trenches. I too give the command to stop all and any firing. We go around our business quite openly, realising that there is not a single shot coming from the other side. This truly is the only time that I sense something like an understanding between us and the enemy. In the position nearby they apparently even got themselves some hot coffee from the French. Everyone seems to be in high spirits. This peaceful atmosphere, however, does not last long. This afternoon already grenades are being fired into our area, smashing hard into the ground both in front of us and behind the line but fortunately without causing any serious damage.[7]

A different attempt at a ceasefire even nearer to Christmas, this time instigated by the Germans, was reported by soldiers of the 15th Reserve Infantry Regiment. On this occasion, it appears that a deliberate desire to celebrate Christmas on a mutual basis with the French was being suggested in the trenches near Reims:

On the evening of 23 December we were suddenly ordered to move forward. The High Command must have expected an attack. But all remained quiet, just as always when we expect a hostile attack. An engineer with the brigade regiment had been collecting lightbulbs for several weeks which he had found in torches that had been cast away, along with dozens of electric batteries. He connected the small bulbs together by a string and with that decorated a Christmas tree. A patrol was later tasked with pinning a note onto a pole of the French wire fence saying the following: 'Tomorrow, we're celebrating Christmas! Don't suspect us of anything nasty.' The same group gingerly carried the little tree and placed it against the enemy wire fence on the 24th towards 9pm. A wire led to the power station in our trench and after the patrol had returned, the engineer switched on the small lamps for them to light up in front of the eyes of the *poilus*.

A magical night descended upon us. Myriads of stars twinkle from the sky. The frost following the heavy downpours has covered the many puddles with a thin sheet of ice. The moon shines. While obscuring the stars in his entourage he bathes the ploughed farmland in a gleaming film of crystals. From the trenches stretching endlessly we hear *'Stille Nacht, Heilige Nacht'*. Not a single shot is fired. *'O du fröhliche, o du selige, gnadenbringende Weichnachtszet'* follows straight on as well as *'Es ist ein Ros' entsprungen'*. Then, once again, calm sets in. A voice calls from the trench on the other side: 'The French took such a liking to your songs that they wish for an encore!' An Alsatian must have translated the request which is being granted ... Midnight is long past. Not a sound disturbs the wounded land. Is it true that here still is a war?[8]

Christmas Eve in many of the sectors manned by French soldiers was thus largely characterised by a gradual diminution of shelling until, by the end of the day, quiet had fallen over much of the front. The principle of reciprocity appears to have been evident, in which one side decided to limit the amount of aggression shown towards their enemy, encouraging the other to respond in kind. A letter from a German soldier based at Romagne-sous-les-Côtes, written on 8 January 1915, recounts how his experience of Christmas Eve mirrored those troops much further north in the British sector.

> On 24 December, at dawn, I woke up to fresh snow covering the battlefield with an icy wind blowing in from the east … During the course of the morning we could still hear rather heavy infantry shelling, nor did we hold back from sending our so-called Christmas messages across to the enemy, but as the afternoon wore on, the firing ceased all together and an eerie silence spread across the entire front. By 10pm at night we gathered around the Christmas tree to finally celebrate Christmas, albeit far from our loved ones and in enemy territory. Our captain held a moving speech which was greeted with a triple 'Hurrah!' for the gracious donors and their gifts from home. This was followed by us singing *'Stille Nacht, Heilige Nacht'* and ending this wonderful day was our exchanging gifts.[9]

Bernhard Lehnert recalled the German love of singing, which ushered in the Christmas celebrations and undoubtedly contributed, as in the British sector, to the mutual desire to temporarily suspend any aggression. Such benevolent intentions were not, however, immediately obvious to their French foe:

> At Christmas 1914 the guards at the trenches sang *'Stille Nacht, Heilige Nacht'*. The minute the first notes had rung through the

night, the French started shooting like mad. They assumed that it was the beginning of an attack, although surely nobody could say that this particular song was inciting war. After a short while they ceased shooting as indeed nothing untoward was happening on our side. They must have finally cottoned on that our singing had something to do with a Christmas celebration and thus remained quiet. Once we had finished singing *'Stille Nacht, Heilige Nacht'*, they intoned the *Marseille*. And that was our Christmas in 1914.[10]

General Otto von Emmich was in command of the German X Army Corps, and similarly remembered how the troops' singing in their trenches on Boxing Day encouraged feelings of comradeship and served to postpone any feelings of aggression. The choice of song was important, though, as when the Germans switched to a more nationalistic choice it proved unpopular with their audience:

26 December 1914: Last night 74th lit Christmas trees near Loivre, right behind the trenches. In the trenches as well, men sang *'Stille Nacht'* and the French let all of this happen without shooting. They permitted everything until *'Deutschland über Alles'* was sung – and that was the only time they fired.[11]

*

Generally speaking, outside of Flanders it was the case that the most each side could hope for was a temporary halt to the usual shelling and sniping. So far the relationship between French and Germans over Christmas 1914 in less aggressive sectors had largely mirrored that which had developed in the British area; festive celebrations were mutually enjoyed and good wishes shouted between the opposing trenches. But when Christmas Day finally came, relations between the French and Germans were not so much marked by a large-scale truce or fraternisation in the manner as had occurred with the British in Flanders, but were rather characterised by a simple lack of fighting. A simple pause, if you will, to celebrate Christmas.

Most areas of the line had to accept that such a temporary ceasefire would prove to be the best improvement they would get to their regular existence. The *Bergische Arbeiterstimme* newspaper printed some of the more interesting letters it received from German soldiers, including the following which was addressed from Lausitz, near Brandenburg in the heart of Germany:

> So, you would like to hear something about Christmas in the field. The mood was rather cheerless and we felt particularly gloomy on Christmas Eve. After all, Christmas is the German family celebration and the pain of feeling lonely or sad at being separated from one's loved ones is felt particularly keenly around Christmas. We have received many gifts and, though we remained in the trenches, we did manage to decorate some Christmas trees. (I will tell you more about the trenches another time.) But spirits were low. The French, it has to be said, were gentlemen and left us in peace.[12]

In a few sectors, however, a degree of proper fraternisation did in fact occur between the French and German soldiers. Broadly speaking, this was a series of short and sweet encounters which were nothing as widespread as the Christmas fraternisation apparent in Flanders. Fritz Ebeling of the 78th Infantry Regiment wrote about such an incident of friendship between the two opposing armies:

> The weather on the morning of the first Christmas Day was nice, clear and cold. A man enlisted with the RIR 15 [15th

Reserve Infantry Regiment] climbs out of his trench which adjoins ours on our left and, lugging a decorated Christmas tree, he waves to the French, who, curiosity in their eyes, look out over the parapet of their positions. Eventually one *poilu* takes heart, walks towards the man and, reaching for the tree which the latter is still holding on to, thanks him and offers him a sip from his flask. A brief shaking of hands, then they part. Emboldened by what they saw, dozens of French also leave their trench and, unarmed, they walk in the direction of the German trenches and there too a large number of Germans have come out from their position. The greeting between the enemies is gallant, gentleman-like: a strong handshake, then an exchange of small gifts, such as chocolate, cigarettes and uniform buttons.

Then a German shrapnel whizzes by at high velocity, meaning it was going to explode beyond the effective kill zone radius and would cause no harm. But it still reminded the Germans that there was a war going on and that they needed to return to base. The French promptly responded by launching four shrapnel which turned out equally harmless. The idyllic interlude had come to an end. On the following night French guns went off once again, targeting German patrols who were roaming the area.[13]

Ralf von Rangow, who was in command of the same 78th Infantry Regiment, went into greater detail about the nature of the meetings in that particular sector on Christmas Day:

> I was woken with the news that the French were standing in groups in front of their trenches waving their caps. They were calling '*Frohe Weihnachten*' ['Merry Christmas'], etc. I reported to Captain Kunze, chief of the artillery battery near Courcy of which I am the commander. He suggested that we shoot, but I ordered that for the time being we would

refrain from doing that as it went against my conscience to disturb the Christmas peace.

When I had arrived at position 101 I was certainly faced with an unusual scene. Along the entire front people had gathered in their hundreds, with French and our men meeting about halfway in the middle between the positions. They were shaking hands, exchanging chocolate, cigarettes, etc. and chatting with each other. Some of our lot knew French, and some on the other side could speak German. Our people had also brought along a small decorated Christmas tree for the French. I have always been aware of the fact that there was no general hatred between us and the French, but it had never really sunk in until that very moment. The madness of this war truly became patently obvious at this sight.

No one who witnessed it will ever forget this image of the first Christmas Day. Nothing can have a more powerful impact on the soul of a soldier than an experience such as this. They didn't hate the enemy. They felt nothing but distaste for murdering human beings, a painful duty they had been ordered to fulfil. They knew full well that the individual *poilu*, the good farmer, the fine tailor and glove maker, that each one of these solid people loves his country, his wife and child and longs to be with them. They were well aware that every soldier on the other side had a home where the beds stood empty in a cosy room. They felt the same pain when in need and when dying – they were all soldiers who deserved respect. We despised our men in their grey coats [i.e. the officers] and we loathed that mindless and foolishly sentimental 'Hurrah!' patriotism as it was portrayed in the newspapers at home.[14]

However, he went on to record that the following night shooting resumed as normal, with the French guns targeting German patrols who were observed in No Man's Land. A further example of meetings in No Man's Land involving the French was given by an artilleryman attached to the 15th Reserve Infantry Regiment:

> On the morning of the 25th somebody places his small tree onto the parapet. Hands, clasping caps, start waving at us. One of our men dares lift himself halfway up to the top, quickly followed by three red-pants [French soldiers]. One after the other appears over the parapet. Eventually, two officers, hands in their pockets, walk towards each other, meet up in No Man's Land, shake each other's hands and strike up a conversation. The French speaks German. Before long the groups grow to about twenty men, all having left their weapons tucked away back in the trenches. Quickly all distrust disappears into thin air and the last men have now emerged. They sniff each other up just like dogs, then shake hands, then they chat in broken English or German. This was a very different encounter from seeing one another as fleeting shadows in the ghostly semi-darkness of the moonlight. The heads of the companies know not what to do ... surely there is no dress code for situations such as these. But then, they decide to grin and bear it ... '*Nous sommes tous des pères de famille. Nous désirons la paix!*' ['We're all fathers to our families. We want peace!'] The men assure me that they had never before so genuinely shaken hands with a friend as they had done just now with the foe.[15]

No Franco-German truce appeared to last for long, although a letter from Privates Schliepman and Kahn, addressed to the Wimmel family of Berlin, does recount one incident of a much longer ceasefire arrangement. Rather than an excuse for mass fraternisation or burial of the dead, this was more of an extension to an existing 'live and let live' arrangement which would not necessarily be linked to a specific moment or purpose.

We are embedded here in the Wöhwald, very close to the French. On Christmas Day, three French came out of their trenches laden with 5 litres of cognac and three bottles of red wine. We, from our side, brought cigars and we then shook hands and with the help of a pocket dictionary we had a good chat. And since then we sort of have an understanding with each other that there will be no shooting when we take a walk between the trenches. When they want to shoot, they first wave to us and then wait until we are safely back in our trenches. This is quite a strange situation and rather comfortable but not sustainable as that would end the war. As well, one doesn't feel like shooting at people with whom we have just shaken hands, and yet war has to continue so that there can be peace. There has to be order.[16]

As artilleryman Rickner recalled, in many cases a reciprocal desire to limit aggression coupled with simple boredom proved enough to encourage benevolent feelings to develop between each army. But any ceasefire understandings which resulted were always relatively minor in scale and limited to certain local areas. They would last only for the immediate Christmas period before the situation shifted back to normal.

It was dull and quiet, we had no ammunition and the French had no ammunition. At Christmas time, on 24 December, our feelings were not at all unfriendly against the enemy. The fraternisation between both lines came to a climax when at about 3 o'clock in the afternoon, about ten or twelve soldiers of our trenches and about the same number of French soldiers came to the middle of the two lines, about 300 metres the trenches were from each other, and met there on the barbed wire and had champagne and wine and cigarettes to exchange. I think they shouted but we had to look through our glasses and couldn't hear any noise really. Then they came back and the next day they did the same, so the day after that we had strict orders not to repeat this fraternisation.[17]

The Belgians too were not averse to sharing an understanding with their enemy as each side celebrated Christmas. Jules Leroy, of the 3rd Infantry Regiment, recalled how the Germans opposite his trenches instigated peace by calling out:

> 'Merry Christmas … we're not shooting tonight.' We responded with a similar message. After some walking to and fro, they put up some lights. We did likewise. Within a short time, the two front lines appeared as if festooned for some festival. Lamps, candles, all lit up in a row. We copied them. And then we sang 'God Save the King' and they chimed in. Indeed, surely they wouldn't have wanted to shoot at an enemy who even sang their own national anthem.[18]

Meanwhile, a Magdeburg newspaper printed the following report, sent to the paper by 'Walter D.':

> A friendly exchange ensued, something one could barely have thought possible and which seemed to border on the fantastical in the eyes of those far removed from the field. There are a number of fir trees floating in the canal and a Belgian, a fabulous tenor, who had previously entertained us by performing *'Wiener Blut'*, took heart, roped the four fir trees together, placed himself on top and, with the help of a telephone wire which we hurled across, we pulled him ashore to our side. This merriment lasted until something like 4.30pm when a Belgian officer ordered that this was it for today as darkness was falling.[19]

Despite such Christmas celebrations going on in the trenches of both sides, as well as in the shared territory between them in some limited cases, most sectors saw the usual military duties being continued under cover of darkness. Gotthold von Rohden, a German officer with the 26th Infantry Regiment, wrote home on Boxing Day from Beaurains to tell his family of how he had narrowly survived a reconnaissance patrol into No Man's Land on Christmas Eve. Far from being the safe space for fraternisation enjoyed by others, the area between the trenches remained a dangerous and potentially fatal place to be:

> On Christmas Eve all of us were more tense than usual as the French, we feared, could well have attempted to attack us. There was a half-moon and the night was beautifully lit – in fact not the best weather to be on patrol. Six volunteers entrusted themselves to my care and as soon as darkness had fallen we began to crawl forwards. The enemy lay dug in but 400 metres away. A mound offering some protection allowed us to approach all the way up to the enemy. While you all blissfully sat around the Christmas tree with the children excitedly waiting for you to lift the snow-white cloth under which were hiding the presents and while duly marvelling at each other's wonderful gifts and while you may have comfortably gathered together later that evening simply to enjoy each other's company, there I was, all tense, inching myself ever closer towards the enemy trench in front of me, conscious of any untoward noise or anything dark lying in my way.[20]

Suddenly the French soldiers appeared to spot the enemy patrol and the 'silent night' was ripped apart by a few sharp shots which reverberated far and wide. The German patrol swiftly took cover but not before one soldier was shot dead and two others seriously wounded. Gotthold hid as best he could in the darkness while a comrade managed to flee back to the German trenches.

> Then French soldiers approached and I honestly felt that my fate was sealed ... But God had different designs for us: watching them closely from where I was positioned, I saw them coming to an abrupt stop just where we had taken cover a few minutes before and then carried on with their conversation at the top of their voices, chatting about the interruption. And there I was, lying right next to the wounded man, trying to make him comfortable by resting his head on my knees and whispering some encouraging words into his ear. While trying to bandage his wound my thoughts wandered to it being Christmas and to many other things ... and it was that very night which had saved us as the Frenchies had obviously decided to celebrate the festivities with alcohol and were merrily singing their *'Marseillaise'* right into the night, followed by 'God Save the King', a Christmas carol and a few war songs. And those back behind us sang Christmas songs, doing so in many voices and including patriotic songs. When one of us offered up a solo, the other side applauded. Quiet as a mouse the Frogs listened to our Christmas carols which you, dear family, were also singing.
> Once I dared hope that the Frogs would indeed not immediately discover us, I started giving some thought as to how we could escape and save our skins even though, at the time, such a possibility seemed quite unlikely. Longingly I observed how the shadows of the bushes became elongated in the pale light of the disappearing moon. I cannot put it in a mere few sentences what I experienced or what went through my mind during the two hours until it had fully

turned dark and a brave orderly had found his way to where we were waiting – not knowing at all where we were lying or if indeed whether we were still there; and it would not have been at all surprising had he turned back 10 metres sooner. But I can tell you one thing for certain: I remained utterly calm and did not fear what was lying ahead of me as I felt that some greater power took care of me. Conscious of being able to offer consolation and protection to another filled me with strength and assurance.[21]

*

Evidence of some form of widespread Christmas Truce happening on the Russian or Serbian fronts is not so easy to find. Christmas is celebrated on 7 January according to the Julian calendar observed by the Russian Orthodox Church, although close enough to the Gregorian tradition of 25 December that any Russian soldiers would have been fully aware of the importance of either date. The local terrain was an important factor in determining the likelihood of fraternisation, since the Flanders trenches and the closeness of each side meant that regular communication between the armies was a more realistic proposition. Some examples of truces held on the Eastern Front can certainly be identified, although these appear to have been mainly small-scale instances of fraternisation and temporary ceasefires which mirrored the Western Front's regular 'live and let live' arrangements at a local level. One example is given by a German soldier writing home on 27 December from Walkalasika in Russian Poland, to offer a description of his unit's Christmas Eve:

> Night has fallen. A deathly silence lies across the battlefield. The air is still and the moon is shining on the farmland. The

dark clouds have receded and lighter ones are taking their place. It seems as if the sky is opening up with a voice calling down: 'Peace on earth!' A simple Christmas tree on the open field should be a reminder to us that it is Christmas. A quiet celebration ensues during which our thoughts travel back to our loved ones who are celebrating far away from us. We chant Christmas carols and remember what it is like at home. Over two hours have been spent with us enjoying a period of calm and peace and now we are all going to sleep. I will never forget this Christmas Eve. Otherwise all is taking its normal course.[22]

Interestingly, while the Western Front witnessed temporary ceasefires and meetings which began in 1914 as a regular occurrence but which then slowly fell out of favour as the war progressed, almost the opposite could be said of the Eastern Front. Letters home from Russian soldiers would regularly mention moments of conversing with their foe and empathising with their shared situation, and these only increased in regularity as the war continued. Such correspondence is also often notable for the criticism contained within it, aimed by ordinary soldiers at their officers and commanders. This largely secret bitterness and frustration would, of course, eventually flare up very publicly in late February 1917 during the Petrograd uprising. When soldiers refused to fire on workers' demonstrations, the insurrection would lead to full revolution and ultimately the overthrow of the Tsarist regime.

It is not surprising, therefore, that fraternisation with the enemy's (largely working-class) soldiery would be seen as a potentially useful seed to encourage the growth of revolutionary spirit. Some commentators have suggested that as the collapse of the Tsarist forces became more likely in Russia, certain German officers actively encouraged their men to fraternise with their Russian enemies, in an identical way to how the Russians themselves would subsequently use fraternisation as a means to destabilise Germany. Writing in *Pravda* in April 1917, Lenin referred to his support of the idea of such fraternisation between Russian soldiers and their German counterparts:

> The capitalists ridicule fraternisations, or they attack them furiously with lies and insinuations, insisting on the way in which the Germans are trying to mislead the Russians. Through their generals and officers, they are threatening severe punishment for anyone guilty of fraternisation ... Yet workers who are informed, semi-proletarians and poor peasants, guided by the accurate instincts of the oppressed classes, are marching in the steps of informed workers, they see fraternisations with the warmest sympathy; it is clear that fraternisations are a route towards peace ... It develops, strengthens, consolidates the feeling of brotherly confidence which unites the workers of the different nations ... It is clear that fraternisation is a revolutionary initiative of the masses, that it signifies the arousing of their awareness, the spirit of courage of the oppressed classes; that it is, in other words, one of the links in the chain which is leading to the people's socialist revolution. Long live fraternisations.[23]

But this long-term effect of fraternisation between Russians and Germans would only bear fruit some years later. As far as Christmas 1914 was concerned, it was the Western Front, and Flanders in particular, which really saw the wide-scale Christmas Truce that would come to be remembered so well.

CHAPTER SIX

Boxing Day and Afterwards

Boxing Day is traditionally considered as an extension to the Christmas holiday, giving people the opportunity to recover from the exertions of the day before, while continuing the possibility of relaxation and enjoyment. It was therefore not so surprising that the Christmas Truce found itself extended in many areas to run through 26 December and in many cases further still, right up to the New Year celebrations and beyond.

For the British soldiers in Flanders, 26 December also happened to be the crossover day when numerous infantry battalions arrived at the front in order to relieve those units which had been in the line over the previous week, and as a consequence many soldiers had their first experience of the truce at this time. 2nd Lieutenant John Wedderburn-Maxwell was serving with the 45th Brigade of the Royal Field Artillery who were based near Laventie and Estairs. He heard the first rumours of a truce on Christmas Day itself:

> I left the wagon line with the horses on Christmas morning and I was told that I was going to the observation post that night, but that I was to come up in time for dinner ... with the other four officers. We had a wonderful Christmas dinner of plum pudding and turkey, I forget how we got hold of it all, and then at dinner Mossie told us that he'd been up that day, with Mickey the vet, and the Germans were all out of their trenches, walking about outside, not mending the wire (that wasn't allowed for some reason) but pumping the water out of the trenches and improving your

own breastworks and so on, and we were doing the same. The Germans had put up on Christmas Eve three or four Christmas trees and they were all singing carols and our people joined in and firing Verey lights.[1]

Boxing Day dawned, and Wedderburn-Maxwell decided to go to see for himself what he had been missing. The temptation to be involved in something which was already being regarded as special enough to warrant particular attention was too strong to resist:

> Next morning nothing was happening and I went up through the communication trenches to the infantry and when I got there I found they were all getting out of their trenches, out of their ditches or behind their breastworks and they were working out in No Man's Land too. Some of them had even met the Germans. There was a party a couple of hundred yards away of our troops and the Germans all fraternising. And so I said, 'I'm going to find out about this,' and I told the infantry to keep an eye on me in case anybody tried any rough business and they'd know what was happening. I went up and I met a small [German] party who said, 'Come along into our trenches and have a look at us.' I said, 'No, I'm quite near enough as it is!' And we laughed and we chafed each other and I gave them some English tobacco and they gave me some German ... and we talked for about half an hour in No Man's Land. And then we shook hands and wished each other luck and one fellow said, 'Will you send this off to my girlfriend in Manchester?' And so I took his letter and franked it and sent it off to the girlfriend in Manchester when I got back!

What did he and the Germans talk about during the fraternisation?

To say how bloody [awful] it was in that mud and how we hated it all and all that and they said, 'We are Saxons, you are Anglo-Saxons. Why are we fighting? The Russians can't fight, the French won't fight, and you're the only people who do fight. And why are we doing it?' They said, 'We had a tremendous victory in Poland and [have] taken a million prisoners ... All that your people tell you is damned lies.'[2]

New battalions of German troops arrived in the trenches on Boxing Day too, to relieve their counterparts who had spent Christmas in the line. Josef Wenzl, of the 16th Bavarian Reserve Infantry Regiment, made his way to the front line in the very early hours of Boxing Day morning and soon noticed that things were not quite the way he expected them to be.

> It was a clear night with the stars and the moon shining, as we advanced towards the trenches. Surely the enemy would spot us and I expected fierce fire and bullets to be hailing down on us. But nobody could describe my surprise when I realised that all remained silent. Not a single shot was fired. As soon as it dawned, the English started appearing on their parapet waving at us. Our men returned the greetings. Gradually more and more soldiers emerged from their trenches and made their way towards each other. Our men planted a Christmas tree on the parapet and rang bells. All of us moved around freely among the trenches, nobody even thought about firing. Bavarians and English, until now sworn enemies, warmly shook hands, chatted with each other and exchanged presents. More and more soldiers, German and English, joined. The better part of our company were soon outside with them. An Englishman approached me and clasped both my hands before then pushing some cigarettes into

them. Another one gave me a handkerchief, a third wrote his name and address into my notebook. A wonderful conversation evolved. One of the English soldiers played on his harmonica while others danced, still others jokingly planted a German helmet onto their head. At some point one of us put up a Christmas tree in between the trenches and immediately each of us had a match ready. Before too long the tree was lit up.[3]

The war diary of the 2nd Battalion, The Queen's (Royal West Surrey Regiment), is particularly interesting for the description it provides of how the Christmas Truce in their sector continued into Boxing Day, having begun on Christmas Day morning. It is also quite unusual for drawing attention to the involvement of German staff officers; such 'red tabs' were rarely seen at the front, at least from the British side.

> Armistice recommenced as arranged at 9am. A large number of staff officers appeared during the day – all were immaculately dressed without a speck of mud on them, mostly in fur lined coats. They furnished us with a list of officers lately taken prisoner and asked that their relatives might be informed. They also promised to try and obtain the release of 2nd Lieutenants Rought and Walmisley, who had been taken prisoners during the armistice on 19th inst. Owing to frost the ground was very hard and the graves were not completed till 1pm, when the chaplain read the burial service in the presence of the digging party, some officers of the Queens and eight or ten German officers. The body of 2nd Lieutenant Bernard, Royal Warwicks, was found and buried. In addition to the 55th Regiment, men of 7th, 15th and 22nd Regiments were noticed. Armistice concluded at 3.30pm.[4]

But in many cases, even in those sectors where the formal period of a ceasefire agreement had now passed, regular firing did not resume and a general reluctance could be discerned by either side to start the war again on proper terms. George Ashurst was asked many years later whether he or any of his fellow British soldiers were ever tempted to seize advantage of such a situation, exploiting the element of surprise by making an attack but thereby breaking an established truce.

> Not in the least, I was more tempted to keep it going for a long time, I was like a lot more [of the other soldiers]. Because it was so pleasant. To get out of that trench, from between those two walls of clay, and walk and run about? It was heaven, that.[5]

It seems logical, then, that many soldiers would endeavour to extend any ceasefire wherever possible, simply through the process of avoiding being the first ones to break such an arrangement. Again we see the importance of the reciprocal agreement for peace and the shared reluctance to be the side to change the situation. Prince Ernst Heinrich, a staff officer based with the General Headquarters of the XIX (2nd Royal Saxon) Corps, recalled how the ceasefire extended in his sector until well after Christmas. Since the arrangement benefitted both sides, by giving them opportunities to repair their trenches without concern that they might be shot, then why would they call a halt to proceedings? The longer the arrangement went on, of course, the more opportunities each side had to fraternise and develop an even more involved relationship with the other. In some extreme cases this rudimentary friendship would actually extend to a greater level of fraternity, even involving regular trips to each other's territory:

At Christmas the Saxons and the English paid each other visits in our respective trenches and offered each other gifts. An officer, whom I knew very well, indeed treated himself every day to a shave on the English side. This idyllic scene which stretched across the sections of two regiments lasted for three weeks. I myself was able to witness this highly unusual situation which took place right in the middle of a war. In this section, total peace reigned and not a single shot was being fired. The officer who accompanied me to the front-line trench told me to cast my eyes across to the other side and so I did. At a distance of some 80 metres I beheld some Tommies look out from over their parapet. The officer loudly shouted, 'Charlie, Charlie,' and after a while I noticed an English soldier climb out from his trench. He approached us as if that was the most natural thing in the world and it truly was more than just a strange feeling to all of a sudden have 'the enemy' face to face and realise that all he has are peaceful intentions to pay a simple visit. Unconsciously I recalled the rather unpleasant greeting which had been introduced back at home at just around this time. It went like this: 'May God punish England.' The response was: 'May God do so.' But back at home this greeting was not well received, and neither was it at the front.

    The English soldier, Charlie, stopped right in front of our trench, saluted as the English tend to do upon seeing a German officer. I said: 'Good morning,' to which he responded, 'Good morning, sir.' He then continued: 'Please follow me.' This Charlie considered himself quite the tour guide and very much liked this role. What then happened was truly sensational. I was quite conscious that I was witness to something extraordinary and not granted to many, which was to encounter the enemy face-to-face in the middle of the war.

In the English trench, which by the way looked exactly the same as ours, a ladder had been propped up and we climbed down to the enemy. We saw several soldiers and sergeants, who greeted us briefly, but didn't see any officers. That was most unusual. Throughout this ceasefire lasting three weeks, we didn't encounter a single officer even though they were entirely aware of the situation. We inspected the English trench – in no way dissimilar to ours with even the obligatory female images pinned up on the walls. They offered us cigarettes and an English soldier said: 'It is a pity to fight, it would be far better to play football. Our regiment against yours.' Typical English and was no doubt meant seriously. The only thing the English didn't permit was photographs being taken as they didn't want any documentation of this unwarlike event which was considered highly undesirable by the top command. After half an hour Charlie brought us back to our trench. Thanking him, we said our goodbyes and he left to return to his side.

On the German side, nothing was done to put an end to the ceasefire as in the west we found ourselves on the defensive, and in the east we were on the offensive, which is the reason that in England any suspension of violence was welcomed. But once this event became known in England, troops were immediately relieved of their duties and replaced. The new regiments received strict orders to shoot any German in sight – and this is exactly what happened. With this, the unofficial ceasefire, which had lasted for three weeks, came to an end.[6]

Those burial parties which had been unable to finish the work that had begun the day before, often resumed the process of recovering and burying their fallen comrades on Boxing Day. Sometimes the process of collecting bodies would reveal further details of the unfortunate men's fate, as shown by the written record of the 20th Infantry Brigade which describes such activity in the Bois-Grenier sector:

> Most of the men reported 'missing' after the fight on the night of 18th–19th are now accounted for. The Germans say they only took ten prisoners. The remainder were all killed or died of wounds. A great many of the dead both British and German were found lying together on the ground between the trenches, silent witnesses to the fierce contest which must have taken place in the darkness. The Germans testified that most of their wounds were caused by bayonets. This is accounted for by the fact that our men's rifles were so clogged up with mud they were unable to fire with them. Means for avoiding this evil have now been adopted. Each man is now being served out with a loose rough canvas bag to slip over the muzzle of his rifle and which is able to be pulled off instantly the rifle is required for use. Even if the rifle is required on the spur of the moment it does no harm to fire it off with the bag still in position on the rifle. Large numbers of men were employed in cleaning out the River-de-Layes in the hopes of being able to drain some of the water out of the trenches. Every day more of the latter are inundated with water by the ever increasing floods.[7]

As such burial jobs were completed, the Christmas Truce fraternisation would often gradually peter out; sometimes quite naturally when the business out in No Man's Land had been completed, but at other times hastened by a mutual agreement over when to resume firing. The situation would also be determined by units being relieved and moving out of the front line, since their replacements may have been less inclined to continue the ceasefire arrangement. Otto Hahn, for one, certainly felt that the cessation of the truce might ultimately be a good thing, as he reflected on the difficulty of preaching 'peace to all men' in the middle of a war:

> The question remains whether one should rejoice or be appalled. I myself am really and profoundly happy about this peace lasting one day. For effect, I make it crystal clear to the men that such a thing is not allowed, not even for the one Christmas Day. It is too dangerous, I say, etc. etc. But deep inside me, I think it is beautiful. But yes, lucky that they are being replaced. It would be hard to shoot at people, or knock them dead with our rifle butts, or pierce their bodies, if one had exchanged cigarettes and food items with them just before. So, this is not what is allowed to happen. Yet, this is what the mood is like around here, and here perhaps it is shown more clearly than elsewhere … so, feelings have to be suppressed.[8]

The following day was Boxing Day, and he wrote to his wife that the truce in their sector was indeed now over:

> For some time our artillery has made it quite clear, and openly so, that this 'Christmas Peace' of ours has come to an end. Heavy weapons are being deployed in close proximity to my quarters, with my windows rattling from the impact. I suspect that this is being done under orders to make it obvious to everyone that the truce is now over for good. Looks to me like the enemy has also returned to his routine and all seems to be back to apple-pie order. Boom, this very second a grenade has exploded just nearby, proving that all is running according to plan.[9]

In some areas, the lifespan of the ceasefire was not so clear cut. Indeed, uncertainty might sometimes remain about whether or not a truce was still in force. An anonymous German officer, in the trenches facing the British 8th Division, commented on how the continued lack of shooting on Boxing Day morning led to questions about whether or not each side were supposed to be resuming the war. Some kind of test was required:

> After noon we lifted a helmet on top of our trench. It took quite some time before a bullet came – far and wide – as a warning. And thus we knew that the war had come again.[10]

In other areas of the front, such as that featured in the following account from Colin Wilson of the Grenadier Guards, the Christmas Truce was definitely being considered as having had its day:

> We, as the Grenadiers, were relieved on Boxing Day and went to the rear ... and there we had our so-called Christmas dinner accompanied by the Prince of Wales, who was then serving with my regiment. And we went back to the line again and of course this fuse was then spreading. By then the General Headquarters behind the line had found out that there was a truce on and that didn't go down very well. So they issued an order that the fraternisation was to cease forthwith and any German soldiers who were seen to leave their trenches for the purpose of fraternising were to be fired upon. Well, we didn't do any firing but somebody did – as soon as the Germans came out on their parapets a blast of machine-gun fire put an end to it. Well, that was that and of course it never occurred again.[11]

*

The military High Command from both sides were indeed becoming aware of the true extent of fraternisation going on in the front lines over Christmas 1914. On Boxing Day, General Sir Horace Smith-Dorrien visited the trenches on an inspection. He had been in charge of the II Corps since the beginning of the First World War but had just received a promotion as commanding officer of the newly created Second Army. The new First Army was under the command of Sir Douglas Haig, who was something of a protégé of Sir John French, the BEF Commander-in-Chief. By contrast, Smith-Dorrien was rather held in contempt by his senior officer. He and French struggled to see eye to eye due to a long-running personality clash, which was perhaps accentuated by their differences in military experience: Smith-Dorrien was an infantryman, while French was from the cavalry.

The possibility of his men becoming involved in some kind of Christmas fraternisation with the enemy had certainly been on Smith-Dorrien's mind in the run-up to Christmas. His instructions of 5 December had already warned against the dangers inherent when 'understandings' were allowed to develop between the British troops and their enemy, and a stern reminder issued by his Chief of Staff on Christmas Day itself had served to repeat to front-line units that their commander's wishes were not being followed.

It was therefore either ironic or fortuitous that the units Smith-Dorrien chose to visit at the front on Boxing Day were not any of those directly involved in the Christmas Truce. It was largely the III, IV and Indian Corps sectors where fraternisation was rife. Yet the general's visit to the trenches still resulted in a great deal of disappointment and frustration on his part, since he witnessed what he regarded as overwhelming apathy among the infantry in the front line. This existing sense of despondency at the situation in the trenches would have been worsened dramatically once he returned to his headquarters, where news was waiting for him of the widespread local ceasefire arrangements still in place in certain sectors. He subsequently issued a confidential memorandum to all the commanders of II Corps which was highly critical of the situation he found during his inspection, with the document ending by drawing particular attention to the Christmas Truce:

> I would add that, on my return, I was shown a report from one section of how, on Christmas Day, a friendly gathering had taken place of Germans and British on the neutral ground between the two lines, recounting that many officers had taken part in it. This is only illustrative of the apathetic state we are gradually sinking into, apart also from illustrating that any orders I issue on the subject are useless, for I have issued the strictest orders that on no account is intercourse to be allowed between the opposing troops. To finish this war quickly, we must keep up the fighting spirit and do all we can to discourage friendly intercourse. I am calling for particulars as to names of officers and units who took part in this Christmas gathering, with a view to disciplinary action.[12]

It is rather easy to guess the immediate reaction of the infantry battalions in the line to such criticism, yet the following specific mention from the war diary of the 2nd Battalion, King's Own Scottish Borderers, serves to indicate the steps taken in response to keep their men busy. Lack of activity was deemed to be the major cause of apathy, which in turn might lead to fraternisation or worse:

> Superior authority expresses dissatisfaction at the fraternising with enemy on Christmas Day. It is forbidden for the future. Also great dissatisfaction is expressed by the 2nd Corps commander at the work done, both offensive

and defensive, in the trenches. Battalions are ordered to do much more spade work, and battalion commanders are ordered to take greater trouble in the matter.[13]

*

As Christmas 'officially' ended with dusk approaching on Boxing Day, there was perhaps a general feeling that the opportune moment for a ceasefire or fraternisation had been and gone. To reinforce this notion, there was also a resumed warning of a potential German attack, obtained from a German deserter who had crossed to the 13th Battalion, London Regiment (The Kensingtons), located near Picantin and Fauquissart. This encouraged the British soldiers to return to their trenches. The war diary of the 20th (Garhwal) Infantry Brigade in the Festubert sector records how they were made aware of this, up to which time they had been experiencing a distinct lack of enemy fire:

> 26 December: [11.55pm] A message was received from Div HQ that 8th Div reported that a deserter had come in tonight stating that an attack was arranged on our lines at 12.15am. Units informed and Leicesters ordered to stand to arms, and move to factory.
>
> 27 December: [12.45am] 58th Rifles ordered to be in readiness and move at a moment's notice. [1.20am] Leicesters ordered to move into houses in Rue des Berceaux should no attack take place by 2am. There was no attack during the night, the Germans being unusually quiet so far as firing was concerned.[14]

Nothing therefore happened, apart from great annoyance being felt by the British units still in the line. Their front-line troops might otherwise have been relieved, as the 2nd Battalion, Northamptonshire Regiment, war diary suggested with barely concealed frustration:

> Suspecting that the Germans might attempt an attack after attempting to lull us into a false sense of security by their friendly advances, great vigilance was enjoined on all ranks and colour was lent to these suspicions by a deserter who came in further along our line and stated an attack was arranged for 12.15am. We were, in consequence, turned out and spent a cheerless night in reserve trenches near Rouge Croix. No attack was made and we returned to our billets at 7am, 27th. Whether the man lied or whether the timely opening of our artillery fire checked the attack cannot be determined.[15]

There were further reasons why the Christmas Truce would come to a natural end. Just as the weather arguably played a role in encouraging the beginning of the truce by being frosty but dry, so its turn for the worse immediately after Christmas led to serious flooding and significantly deteriorating conditions in the trenches. A sprinkling of snow on Boxing Day turned into sleet by the evening, while the following day was largely full of rain. A violent storm on the night of 28–29 December brought an even worse state of affairs, including thunder, hail and high winds. Priority suddenly had to be shifted to improving the soldiers' living conditions, and any thoughts of fraternisation out in No Man's Land were certainly halted.

However, since the urgent task of properly repairing the trenches and pumping out excess water was shared by both sides, a continued ceasefire would help enormously to complete this activity. With British, French and Germans all sharing the same living conditions and facing identical weather, it made complete sense to disregard instructions to continue aggression while other things closer to home needed to be addressed. The truce would therefore continue in some areas, but largely as a ceasefire – without the fraternisation which had distinguished Christmas. The war diary of the 1st Battalion, Somerset Light Infantry, provides a useful record of the days between Christmas and New Year and the activity undertaken by that unit, showing how the ceasefire continued to provide opportunities for improving the condition of the trenches in that sector:

> 26 December: Truce still continued – no firing of any description. Spent the day strengthening defences and working at the new breastworks in supporting line.
> 27 December: Truce still continued.
> 28 December: The truce continued today but about 8pm the Germans sent over to say they were going to continue firing at midnight. However no shots were fired in our vicinity.
> 29 December: Truce still continued and opportunity was taken of it to strengthen the defences considerably.
> 30 December: Truce still continues … Good progress made today on the breastworks behind right trench; also supporting breastworks. The Germans sent in the following message to the Left Trench this morning: 'Dear Camerades, I beg to inform you that is [sic.] forbidden us to go over to you, but we will remain good camerades. If we shall be forced to fire we will fire to [sic.] high. Please tell me if you are English or Irishmen. Offering you some cigars, I remain yours truly camerade, X.Y.' No answer was given to this communication.
> 31 December: The Germans celebrated the New Year with great vigour. Trumpets were sounded and other instruments played and there was much singing. They also had lanterns hung on their wire entanglements. At

11pm they fired a *feu-de-joie* [celebratory gunfire] over our heads. This was taken by our guns to mean an intended attack and they started shelling.[16]

As this final diary entry reminds us, the next opportunity for potential celebrations following Christmas was the traditional welcoming in of the New Year. The chronicles of the 1st Battalion, Rifle Brigade, based in the St Yves sector, provide an unusual example of a very specific ceasefire arrangement sought by the Germans opposite their position. Hostilities in that area had not properly resumed since Christmas, with a ceasefire continuing despite a lack of outward fraternisation between the troops. Indeed, the Rifle Brigade were enjoying such good terms with their enemy that the Germans would send over messengers on a regular basis to warn them if they were forced to recommence hostilities due to orders received from higher up the chain of command. The appetite for friendship appeared to remain strong among the Germans, as several times the British had to walk out to tell the German patrols to keep further away, rather than warning them in ruder fashion. On 30 December a note was received from a German officer seeking a more formal temporary armistice, presumably linked to the imminent New Year celebrations to mark the beginning of 1915:

The acting general command has given orders (as follows):

1. An armistice for the purpose of burying the dead will take place on 31.12.14 from 10am until 2pm (German time) if a written assent to the underwritten conditions is previously here given by the acting (competent) English commanders.
2. A boundary line, to be determined on by the German and English officers, is to be fixed which may in no

circumstances be crossed. All ranks of the English army are to avoid coming over to this (German) side of the line. The dead are to be carried over by German soldiers where necessary.

3. During this period neither side is to fire on the whole front comprising the east edge of the Bois Ploegsteert from St Yves–Ivgheer. Nor is the artillery (to fire) into any of the ground behind the lines (including the ground east of the Lys).
4. The officer in command of the infantry and artillery in the sector in question must declare his assent to these conditions in writing, and have it sent back again to the (German) officer who sent it over originally.
5. If this statement of agreement is not back in possession of the German officer by 8am, 31.12.14 (German time), the truce on 31.12.14 cannot be observed.

(signed) Oberst Thorn
despatched 4.20pm[17]

It seems that on this occasion the offering of a temporary truce was refused, for the war diary does not mention any special ceasefire being agreed for 31 December or immediately afterwards.

In other areas the truce extended into 1915, with Christmas festivities merging into those celebrations to welcome in the New Year. Rifleman Graham Williams was back in the trenches near Armentières, having enjoyed a brief rest period in reserve just after Christmas. Having already experienced the festive ceasefire and fraternisation, Williams might be forgiven for thinking that the situation at the front would have returned to normal by now. But he was about to find out that the situation for him would become even more bizarre than before!

On New Year's Eve we were in the trenches again, and I was engaged on a very unpleasant job with two other men, trying to pump out a disused communication trench which was full of water and liquid mud, with a very inadequate pump. We were wearing gumboots and unless you kept on moving your feet you gradually sank in until it was over the top of the gumboots. So I was very pleased when a runner came along with a message for me, asking me to go up to the front line as I was wanted to act as interpreter again. So I got to the front line and found a very drunk German standing in a trench, right up to his knees in water, leaning against a parapet, waving a bottle of beer in each hand: *'Trinken,trinken! Neujahr, neunzehn fünfzehn!'* ['Drink, drink! New Year 1915!'] and our officer was in front of him trying to persuade him to go, but the officer couldn't speak German and this bloke couldn't understand English. So that's why he wanted me to interpret. He said, 'Well, you must tell this chap that he's got to go back to his trenches.' So I told him, but *'Nein, nein, trinken, trinken,'* so the officer said, 'Well, this chap can see our trenches, can see what a very bad condition they're in, and also see how few of us are manning the trench, and he can go back and make a report on them.'

But personally I thought in any case that the German trenches were bound to be just as bad as ours with the same waterlogged ground. That was long before the days of deep German dugouts and things. And also they could pretty well judge how many of us there are from the number they've seen walking about during the last few days. The same as we had formed a pretty good estimate on their strength. And then on top of all that this bloke was obviously far too drunk to make any report on anything.

So our officer said, 'Well as he's seen our trenches we really ought to take him prisoner, but I don't really want to do that, it might upset the Germans and stop this truce.' So I explained this to the chap, and told him he ought not to be there at all. He still refused to go, so he said, 'Ask him if he wants to become a prisoner.' So I did and he said, *'Ah gott, nein nein, trinken, trinken'*. So I thought it's pretty obvious we shan't be able to persuade him to go, so I told the officer, 'I don't think there's much use, sir, I don't think we can persuade him, he won't go.' So he said, 'We'll have to take him then.' So he detailed another chap and myself to take him back to his lines. We managed to haul him up the parapet and we each took hold of one of his arms and led him back across No Man's Land. There he was, in between, staggering along and singing very bawdy songs at the top of his voice until we got up to the German wire where there was a gap that he'd come through obviously. I said to the other chap with me, 'Well I don't think we'll go any further, if we get into their trench they might want to keep us there.' So we put this chap heading in the right direction, wished him a Happy New Year and left him to it![18]

The particular sector of the line in which Williams was serving proved to be where the Christmas fraternisation would last for the longest continual period:

In our sector [the Truce] lasted for over a week, because we started on Christmas Eve and it was still in force on New Year's Day when we were relieved in the evening, it was still in force then. I think it came to an end the next day, but I'm not sure. But it had been arranged that whichever side had to break the truce first would give warning first of all, and also when it was definitely decided to end the truce, to fire a few shots in the air first of all to give everybody the chance to get back into their trenches again. And although we weren't in the trenches at the time – the Somersets were in the same trenches then – the Germans did carry this out. They sent a message during the daytime that the automatic pistol – they meant the machine gun – would fire at such and such a time and it did, in the air, well over the heads of the trenches. Rumour has it that our adjutant was walking up Ploegsteert Wood at the time and he had to take cover because these bullets from a machine gun nearly got him, and they were just stray bullets. And the point about that was that he had the reputation of being not exactly frightened, but very careful of himself.[19]

Karl Aldag similarly recalled a New Year's Truce, although this was ostensibly only called for in order to collect and bury the bodies identified as still lying out in No Man's Land. Presumably this particular sector of the front line had not seen burial parties out in force during the Christmas period, as had certainly happened elsewhere.

> New Year's Eve was quite strange around here. An English officer came over carrying a white flag and requested a ceasefire from 11am to 3pm so they could bury the dead. (Shortly before Christmas we had experienced some heavy fighting in this area which cost the English a large number of dead and very many of their men were taken prisoner). It was granted. It's nice to no longer see the corpses lying there spread in front of you. The ceasefire was extended. The English left their trenches, came up to the middle and exchanged with our men cigarettes and cans of tinned meat and photos and said that they no longer wanted to engage in firing.
>
> Thus, complete calm set in which all seemed somewhat strange. Here we are, with the enemy and us walking up on top of the parapet and neither of us in any hurry to return into our trenches. We felt that this couldn't continue in the

long run and so we told the officer that the men should please return to the trenches as we would begin to shoot. The English officer apologised and said that, regrettably, his men no longer wished to obey. The soldiers no longer felt like waging war. They no longer wanted to be lying in their wet trenches. France was ruined long ago. Of course, we didn't shoot. In truth, their circumstances are much worse than ours are on this side: it is filthier over there, they are dirtier, they have run out of water and they have a large number of sick and wounded men to care for. Their soldiers are all mercenaries, so they just go on strike, plain and simple. Of course we didn't shoot, seeing as our trench too (the one leading right from the firing line into the village) is continuously full of water and it really suits us to take walks along the parapet without fearing for our lives. Is the entire English army on strike, we asked, and does this strike throw a spanner into the London gentlemen's works?[20]

By now, it was a common expectation for each side to seek souvenirs of their fraternisation together, and the German officers all signed their names in an album that the English provided for this purpose. Yet their time together in No Man's Land was not to last for much longer:

> An English officer came over informing us that he had been given orders 'from above' to target our trenches: would we please be good enough to take cover? And, indeed, the (French!) artillery opened fire but we suffered no losses. We had agreed on the time – midnight – when both sides fired a few salvos. It was a cold evening. We sang some of our well-known tunes and those on the other side applauded (we only lie some 60 to 70 metres apart from each other). We played on the harmonica and others accompanied our music by singing. Then I called across, asking whether they

also had some instruments on them; so they came up with a bagpipe and played their lovely elegiac Scottish melodies; it was the Scots Guard with their fluttering skirts and naked legs and they also sang along. At midnight the salvos on both sides came crashing through the air. Our artillery also let off a few shots, I am not sure what they were aiming at, and [as] flares crackled into the sky as if they were fireworks, we swung torches back and forth and shouted 'Hurrah'. We had brewed ourselves a grog which we enjoyed while cheering the Kaiser and greeting the New Year. It was a New Year's celebration as one only knows from peacetime.[21]

Rather than following the path of peace, some units appear to have signalled the New Year by deliberately firing volleys at the enemy, substituting the traditional fireworks with shellfire and sniper bullets. So it is hardly surprising under these circumstances that a widespread rerun of the Christmas Truce would not happen on New Year's Day. The German soldier Richard Dehmel recalled his unit's attempts to celebrate the New Year opposite the French trenches:

> Even when we made music around midnight on New Year's Eve and sang some fun songs while firing off some rockets into the sky, we were not disturbed in the least. At the end, we climbed up onto the rampart and shouted across in loud voices: 'Bonne année' but nobody responded, not with a call, nor with a bullet.[22]

By this time any momentum for the continuation of a wide, large-scale truce was spent. Similarly, any possibility of a spontaneous reoccurrence of fraternisation had been exhausted by other factors such as the deteriorating weather and the increasing awareness of the senior commanders from both sides of what was going on at the front. Occasional small truces would still be held on a semi-regular basis in order to collect wounded and bury the dead. But rather than being an organised and widespread ceasefire, the situation now was more akin to the 'live and let live' mentality of inertia – the avoidance of deliberate aggression in order to allow the troops a breathing space to concentrate their efforts upon other priorities. The two areas where this continued to be most prevalent were Ploegsteert Wood, which already enjoyed a reputation as a 'cushy' sector, and the area of the line further south of Armentières, round Laventie and Fleurbaix. Peace continued in these sectors well into January 1915, and in some cases was still prevalent in February and March. In areas such as these, the fighting spirit seems to have evaporated to a significant degree.

We will look at the longer legacy of the Christmas 1914 ceasefires and fraternisation in a later chapter, but first it might be helpful to examine in greater detail exactly why the Christmas Truce occurred in the first place. Was it truly a spontaneous eruption of friendliness and goodwill, or were there deeper reasons already in existence which provided the inspiration?

CHAPTER SEVEN

Causes

We have seen how temporary ceasefires and fraternisation were by no means unknown throughout the initial months of the First World War, and it could certainly be argued that the smaller-scale 'live and let live' mentality already prevalent set the conditions for a more widespread phenomenon to occur at the end of the year involving many thousands of soldiers. In these terms, the Christmas Truce of 1914 was by no means a spontaneous event but rather a manifestation of conditions already bubbling near the surface for quite some time. Indeed, rather than being regarded as a single large-scale truce, perhaps the event should be better seen as a series of smaller arrangements which led to the promulgation of a wider ceasefire. Perhaps the key question to ask is not so much why the Christmas Truce occurred when it did, but rather why the fighting *resumed* and similar truces did not happen more widely and increasingly often? The simple answer is that they *did* continue, though in a significantly less obvious way. But first let us look in more detail at the direct causes of the ceasefire and fraternisation at the very end of 1914.

To begin with, we should recognise that there were special factors in the case of the Christmas Truce. It is no coincidence at all that the largest and most widespread example of fraternisation seen during any modern war should happen over the period of the year's most important religious festival and public holiday. Christmas encouraged seasonal feelings of goodwill and promoted the central Christian tenet of 'peace to all men'. Annual yuletide traditions also served to remind people of the importance of friends and family, based around the sharing nature of Christmas time. With all of these ideas being uppermost in the minds of soldiers as 25 December approached, the possibility of a ceasefire or understanding with their enemy would have seemed as realistic a notion as it could ever be. It was also relatively early on in the war, when romantic ideas of a 'last chance for peace' were already circulating back home and being spoken about prominently by religious leaders.

The German soldier Rupert Frey of the 16th Reserve Infantry Regiment felt that the religious importance of the day was certainly the key to understanding the Christmas Truce:

> What had motivated the people to leave their trenches and come over to us? Was it an unconscious desire for peace? Was it a night filled with thoughts about Christmas, was it the magic of this sacred night? What had compelled the enemy? Silent night, holy night, never before have you been so real, so tangible, despite us being here, in the midst of the horrors of the war! And if, in our case, the good tidings should find fulfilment 'May there be peace on earth for those who are filled with good will'. If, indeed, good fortune might grant us a safe return to our homeland, we will never forget Christmas 1914 in the field.[1]

Artillery officer Reginald Thomas was with the 45th Brigade of the Royal Field Artillery, part of the British 8th Division, and similarly believed that the unique effect of Christmas time was very important to the establishment of the ceasefire:

> There was a feeling in the air, we can't go on killing each other today, you know what I mean? And it was a mutual feeling on

both sides, but we had no bitter feeling against the Germans. I never had that and I never met anybody [who did].[2]

A German soldier from Traunstein, writing home on Boxing Day, was also under no doubt as to the special nature of the event:

> Close to Messines it even came to a gathering between some of our men from the 16th Section and the English. Together they celebrated Christmas Eve, exchanged gifts, shook each other's hands to then hurry back into their trenches. Oh Christmas, how divine you are, how you soften men's hearts. A Christmas spirit fills my soul and I can barely put this sentiment into words. Even if a warrior thinks of his loved ones at all times, during Christmas Eve the memories are more powerful still.[3]

With both Germany and Britain being overwhelmingly Christian nations, it was perhaps inevitable that the most important religious celebration of the year would interfere with the normal course of events. The German war correspondent Walter Oertel recognised the great significance of the holiday, realising that even non-believers would regularly celebrate the annual Christmas festival as one of the most important dates on the calendar.

> Sitting peacefully by candlelight, we may not waver in our wish to remain fighters. While it is difficult for us to have 'the great holy peace' exist alongside 'the great holy war', seeing as we are creatures of thought it couldn't be otherwise and, indeed, who knows which of them reigns supreme.[4]

However, the unique scale of the 1914 experience suggests that it is much more likely to have been a combination of various other elements which encouraged such a widespread fraternisation at that particular time. These factors were the same as those which inspired the earlier ceasefires and fraternisation which we have recognised as having occurred since the beginning of the trench war, and it is therefore worth looking in detail at these myriad reasons which combined to create the Christmas Truce.

The cause which was arguably more important than anything else when influencing the state of mind of the soldiers at that particular moment was the common desire to improve one's existence, if only for a short period of time. Life in the trenches was characterised by almost constant danger, with the threats from snipers, shelling or even sickness being regular companions to a soldier every day. Troops in the front line would have been understandably keen to enhance their well-being and, wherever possible, alleviate the mental stress which was caused by being put in constant danger. But any attempt to improve the situation was always seriously limited by the fact that trench inhabitants were under the constant vigilance of their enemy. Just to raise one's head above the parapet might provoke instant retaliation, let alone the danger faced in undertaking proper improvement work to trenches and dugouts. The only sure-fire method of obtaining a respite from immediate danger, and providing the opportunity to improve living conditions, would therefore be to halt the war, albeit temporarily.

As the end of 1914 approached, circumstances combined to make the possibility of some kind of local ceasefire agreement a more realistic prospect. The nature of the weather changed as autumn began to move very definitely into winter, and as conditions grew colder and wetter they only served to highlight the need to concentrate on matters other than the fighting of a war. Heavy rainfall caused widespread flooding in the trenches, with the Flanders sector being particularly susceptible due to the nature of the already boggy land. This in turn necessitated greater work to be done on maintaining the trench defences, to ensure that they were still inhabitable despite the increasing flooding and mud. Christmas itself was marked by a dry but frosty spell, which proved to be an opportune moment to allow improvement works to be carried out more successfully.

As if conditions in the Flanders fields were not bad enough, there was the added issue of the large number of dead bodies lying in close proximity to the living. The recent Franco-British offensive in that area during the first half of December had resulted in a significant number of casualties whose bodies had never been recovered, and which remained in the dangerous No Man's Land between the two armies.

It is therefore logical to regard the Christmas Truce as a practical exercise in creating a ceasefire in order to undertake important work to improve the soldiers' immediate living conditions. Any truce is by necessity a two-sided agreement, but with both sides experiencing exactly the same challenges and difficulties, it made perfect sense to pursue a mutually beneficial solution. Graham Williams certainly remembered the implementation of the truce in such terms:

> In some places apparently [the truce] was frowned upon, but in our sector anyway, as far as Brigade was concerned, it was encouraged because it enabled us to do a lot of work on the trenches and also on various fortifications which were being built in Ploegsteert Wood without the nuisance of continual machine-gun fire, which they did every now and then from time to time on the wood. So I mean as far

as we were concerned ... the truce was a good thing and we wanted it to continue, we didn't want to stop it at all.[5]

Rather than being a politically incited socialist uprising against authority, or even a spontaneous rebellion of the human spirit against the principle of war, the Christmas Truce was at heart much more rooted in the practical advantages gained when downing weapons for a brief time, making sensible use of the opportunities that this presented while enjoying the sentimentality of the Christmas period. Prince Ernst Heinrich, the Duke of Saxony, discussed Christmas 1914 in his memoirs which were published after the war. In September of that year he had become batman in the General Headquarters of the XIX (2nd Royal Saxon) Corps, based at Reims and Lille. He too had no doubt at all that one of the main causes of the Christmas Truce was the fact that men from both sides were concerned with improving their living conditions, more than any other reason:

> Flanders is a very flat area in the Low Countries with high ground-water levels. The rainfall during the winter months is considerable. And when the trenches were being built, especially south of Armentières, we hit water after barely digging to any significant depth. The only option both sides took recourse to was to build the walls which were facing the enemy ever higher. Shortly before Christmas the rainfall was unusually heavy with the water in the dugout rising and special measures were required so that the soldiers could remain in their positions. However, the works could not be carried out without exposing oneself to the enemy. Thus risks had to be taken and both sides did so. It just happened, without any previous arrangements, that neither side shot at their opposite. What then evolved happened

very quickly. Everyone worked away, no guns were used, we looked, waved at each other and exchanged cigarettes.[6]

An officer of the 55th (6th Westphalian) Infantry Regiment also recalled how none of the participants in the Christmas Truce really expected a lasting peace, but rather just made the most of the momentary ceasefire in order to gain immediate benefits:

> Nobody needed to fear that a separate peace with England would have been forged then and there in Flanders – though from the political perspective it wouldn't have been a bad idea at all. But we welcomed the ceasefire not least because the many corpses disappeared and they certainly had badly affected fighting morale.[7]

*

The Christmas Truce was therefore an explicit acknowledgement that both sides shared the same challenges and desires, with the front-line troops feeling enough empathy towards each other that they were willing to halt the war for their combined benefit. But what exactly were these shared issues which brought both sides together and would lead to the mass fraternisation at Christmas time?

Food of course is always highlighted as one of the most important aspects of military life, since the strength of a soldier's morale is directly linked to his hunger. A starving soldier is unlikely to respond well to orders from above. Shared empathy thus existed between the soldiers from each side with regard to both food and water, since they were essential requirements; as such, the basic need for food and sustenance was mutually respected. Rations were often delivered at roughly the same time to both British and

German trenches, and mealtimes were similarly observed by a lack of deliberate sniping. Of course this was not *always* the case, since in more aggressive sectors it might have been more likely that mealtimes would actually be targeted as moments of obvious activity in the opposite trench. But it was much more common for the troops to recognise and respect each other's human needs. Graham Williams recalled such an example which highlights how important the 'live and let live' mentality could sometimes prove to be:

> In front of the Somerset trenches which we occupied then, the German trenches were only about 40 yards away from ours at that point and in between the trenches there was a derelict farmhouse there which had a pump, which was in working order. And we used to go and fill our water bottles with this pump and the Germans evidently did the same because we used to hear it clanking when we knew none of our people were there. If we wanted to go we used to always listen first of all carefully before we went to take out water bottles to be filled to see if the Germans were there, and they obviously did the same. But we both used to use this pump.[8]

Another characteristic of military life is the sheer boredom of following orders which often involve routine tasks, whether they happened to be cleaning one's rifle, repairing defences by filling sandbags or standing for hours on sentry duty. Such tasks of tiresome regularity were tempered only by the camaraderie with one's fellows, typified by many hours spent chatting with comrades or enjoying group singalongs. Where trenches were dug close to the enemy lines, it was quite possible to hear the other side talking and laughing. The natural extension to this would therefore be to include the enemy in the conversation too – at first through shouted exchanges, then perhaps by notes being thrown across or held up. Ultimately, in some sustained cases, this would lead to direct fraternisation in person.

Interestingly, the attitude of the ordinary soldiers towards their more senior officers might sometimes mean that a greater kinship was felt with their enemy in the opposite trenches, rather than a sense of obedience to their military superiors. The real distinction in trench life was not so much determined by social status, but rather down to whether a soldier was in the front lines (as an active fighter) or behind the lines (as a passive participant). In this way, Leslie Walkinton recalled how the Christmas Truce was an opportunity for the ordinary soldiers to express themselves without fear of retaliation from their higher commanders. In a way, it was a minor rebellion:

> Our own officers were a bit scared, they thought they'd be court-martialled and all that. Fraternising with the enemy was of course against military rules. We thought it was a damn good joke. We were under discipline all the time, you know, and it was one way of laughing at one's superiors. There was nothing they could do about it, I mean if a brigadier had come and tried to order us back we would have laughed at him I think. Anyway, they had the nous to keep away.[9]

Inherent in the attitudes expressed by those in the front-line trenches was the idea that there were recognised 'rules of the game' which existed and that both sides needed to follow. Although now largely seen as an outdated concept, the idea that there was such a thing as gentlemanly conduct during a war was still a popular one among the combatants and led to a certain degree of mutual respect between them. Such 'rules of the game' would largely be promulgated by those seasoned veteran soldiers who were part of the regular army and who were particularly prevalent within the BEF at this early stage of the war. They would play an important part in training up and influencing new recruits. In the British Army alone, by December 1914 the regular BEF had been supplemented by fourteen battalions of Territorial Force volunteers and, despite their great inexperience, these men would be rapidly brought up to speed by the established regular NCOs and officers. Otto Gabcke was a German officer in the 158th (7th Lotharingian) Infantry Regiment, and mentions this 'gentlemanly' aspect of war:

> On Christmas Eve we were very surprised. For two days our enemies were perched on the parapet. They no longer fired any shots and just roamed around the ramparts and the field. Our boys were quite attracted by such gentlemanly behaviour and immediately followed suit.[10]

Connecting this further with the reasons why truces and fraternisation were such regular occurrences, we should recognise that an important element of the 'rules' of trench warfare was the idea of reciprocity – the moral belief that it was deemed correct and appropriate to offer one advantage in exchange for another. If peace was offered by the enemy in the form of a ceasefire, then it was only right and proper to accept it and share the benefits. Limited violence from one side would invariably lead to further understandings and exchanges developing; souvenirs and food might be swapped by each side, while vocal exchanges involving humour, conversation, music and song were equally common. An adjunct to this was the idea that basic friendliness could prove to be valuable as a sort of 'advance investment' for the future. The prospect of becoming a prisoner of war at some future date may well have been in the minds of many soldiers, in which case such friendly compassion practised today might prove a wise tactic in order to receive similar treatment from their enemy in due course.

Throughout the war Ludwig Renn served as an officer in a prestigious Saxon Guards Regiment. His first book, *Krieg*, which appeared in 1928 and brought him wide acclaim, recognised the importance of simple communication in terms of exchanging gifts, thereby generating friendship:

> In such a situation where two enemies happen to confront each other and with neither of them being a hero, but simply two soldiers who actually fear each other, then they tend to behave quite differently. In order to calm down the hostile 'other', one offers something to the other. For instance, a cigarette. Out of opportunism they then forge a friendship. Does one really have to hate someone (just because) you wage war against each other?[11]

Linked to the reciprocity idea was the group dynamic of the trenches. Rather than acting as individual fighters, trench inhabitants would almost always operate as a group, making shared decisions and following mutual orders. Any decision to restrict aggression in the hope of receiving similar treatment from the enemy would therefore have to be made at a group level. Pressure from his compatriots often existed for a soldier not to endanger everybody else by displaying unnecessary aggression towards the enemy, since this would likely lead to retaliation which would harm the group. The system of trench warfare relied on solidarity among soldiers for successful outcomes in terms of both safety and protection, and this naturally influenced limited aggression as a group. In other words, at its simplest level, the more soldiers who decided to limit their aggression, the greater the chance for a truce to occur and for multiple soldiers to be involved in fraternisation.

We should recognise, however, that it is difficult to discuss trench warfare except in generalities. Despite the advantages of communication with the enemy and recognition of 'gentlemanly' conduct, there was also always the satisfaction in getting one over on your opponent. Indeed, soldierly conduct could be interpreted in many different ways. Oberleutnant Albrecht Ludwig Volz of the 126th (8th Württemberg) Infantry Regiment described in his diary how aggression could sometimes be considered as 'fair game':

> Observed for quite some time a group of French officers leisurely walking some 100 metres behind where they were positioned along the edge of the forest, having a smoke and chatting among themselves. This made me make up my mind right then and there. Considering such behaviour unseemly, I thought it best to correct the situation quickly and did so with the help of a machine gun I had requested to be brought to me. Peace came to an abrupt end.[12]

Almost all personal testimony which describes the establishment of a ceasefire draws attention to the importance of communication with one's enemy. Direct communication between opponents proved invaluable in hastening any opportunity for full-on fraternisation, while sectors in which trench lines were dug closely together would generally lead to greater communication between the two sides and a higher likelihood of a truce. A desire for a truce or ceasefire was invariably made verbally, whether by holding up signs above the trench parapet or shouting to one's opponents. Written messages scrawled on a board and raised above the trenches to be viewed by the other side were fairly common, as Albert Moren of the 2nd Battalion, The Queen's (Royal West Surrey Regiment), recalled:

> The trenches were almost within throwing distance until they used these grenades, the trenches then got far apart. We could hear the Germans talking at night, singing and everything. We used to say, 'I wonder what Jerry's thinking, I wonder what Jerry's doing' … we were so close in those days. We were so close we threw tins over to them and they threw things back. You'd get a zigzag line, one part you'd be a long way away and another place where there'd be a sort of protruding trench sometimes you'd be quite near to each other. Bully beef and jam and biscuits, things like that and they're throwing things back. It wasn't done regular but an occasional sort of thing, naturally. They used to shout across, 'Englander, Englander', you know, and we used to say, 'good old Jerry' and things like that.[13]

The language barrier was not so great a problem as might first be supposed. Generally speaking, not so many British soldiers spoke German, but quite a few Germans spoke passable English. Some Germans had spent time in the United Kingdom before the war, either for education or employment. 2nd Lieutenant John Wedderburn-Maxwell recalled the excellent English spoken by those Germans whom he mixed with on Boxing Day:

> One was an American, another was a waiter at the Ritz, there were several of them that talked to me that talked quite a bit of English. Of course before the first war nearly all the barber shops in this country were Germans.[14]

In his important book on the 'live and let live' system during the First World War, Tony Ashworth remarks that 'evidence from sources suggests that tacit truces emerged on all ... fronts except Gallipoli'.[15] Perhaps it was the significant difference between the Turkish language and culture and those of the Allies in that theatre of war which explains why truces were rarely if ever established during that campaign. Only one significant temporary armistice was established at Gallipoli, on 24 May 1915, and that was very strictly controlled and arranged with the single purpose of burying thousands of bodies following a particularly unsuccessful offensive. On the Western Front, however, Germany and the other European nations had many more similar customs and shared heritage, which in turn only encouraged empathy and understanding.

However, sometimes it might be the case that significant cultural differences existed within each single nationality, which might directly influence whether they were likely to go along with the idea of fraternisation. We have already noted that evidence suggests that Saxon or Westphalian troops seemed to be much more likely to express sociable tendencies than Prussians, who had a reputation for being more militaristic. These different attitudes go some way towards explaining why certain sections of the Flanders front did not become involved in the Christmas Truce. Lieutenant Wedderburn-Maxwell certainly thought as much:

> Prussian officers were such a tough lot, a ruthless lot, had they been in that situation they would probably not have allowed it. You see on some occasions in war one funny little man – may be a private soldier, may be an NCO, might be an old officer – will take the lead in something. And it's possible that one of our people, seeing a German, waved across with a white flag (we weren't allowed white

handkerchiefs, only khaki ones) and drew a response from the other side. Or the Germans might have done the same. It can evolve from one man's brain, I've seen it happen in a disaster with terrible casualties and things, one man will step out and take charge, a man just thought of as an ordinary driver looking after two horses and there he was, something in him, a bit of leadership exploded at the critical moment.[16]

This leads us to consider the general feelings which each side had towards their respective enemy. Early on in the war the aggression and antagonism which became such a strong characteristic by the end of the conflict was not so evident. A clear difference in attitude can also be identified between the protagonists in the trenches and civilians back home. The beginning of the war had seen a remarkable amount of anti-German propaganda which proved immensely influential on the minds of the Allied nations, especially in terms of the allegations of German atrocities against women and children during the initial invasion of Belgium. Such allegations would only develop further into greater circulation as the war progressed.

Atrocity stories were often received awkwardly by soldiers in the trenches, since their first-hand experience of the enemy did not always match up with propagandist depictions. They largely had the same trench experience as their German equivalents, suffering the same weather and flooded trenches, the same challenges to stay alive in such primitive conditions. All this served to emphasise their united humanity, while opportunities for communication helped to bring the two armies even closer together. Enmity provides a justifiable motive for aggression, yet realisation that your enemy is not totally evil, nor entirely different from oneself, serves only to discourage violence.

While the main causes of the Christmas Truce were arguably practical ones, we should recognise the existence of human feelings which were not attached to territory, nation or government but which were shared by all soldiers and went beyond the common Christmas traditions. Plunged into a war largely built on political panic emanating from the top, the troops from both sides momentarily emerged from their military and hierarchical constraints to enjoy a moment of individuality. This involved, as Professor Michael Schober has suggested, the soldiers sharing instead of shooting; enjoying sport rather than being drilled in it; being moved by music as opposed to marching; and being visible to each other out in the open, rather than being hidden in the confines of a trench. 'For a moment, they were able to be civilians in charge of their actions.'[17]

The language of the trenches is an interesting aspect which reveals how each side felt about the other. The adoption of nicknames such as 'Fritz' or 'Tommy' tended to be used almost affectionately and rarely as expressions of hate. Although many British soldiers still blamed Germany for the atrocities they were alleged to have committed, such things were often considered to be the fault of the Prussians or the German leadership, as opposed to the 'decent' Saxon soldiery.

> Hatred of the enemy, so strenuously fostered in training days, largely faded away in the line. We somehow realised that individually they were very like ourselves, just as fed up and as anxious to be done with it all. For the most part, the killing that was done and attempted was quite impersonal.[18]

Lieutenant Bruce Bairnsfather served with the 1st Battalion, Royal Warwickshire Regiment, based in the St Yves sector. Although a participant in the Christmas Truce, he would become better known much later on as a cartoonist who depicted life in the trenches.

> This was my first real sight of them at close quarters. Here they were – the actual, practical soldiers of the German army. There was not an atom of hate on either side that day; and yet, on our side, not for a moment was the will to war and the will to beat them relaxed. It was just like the interval between the rounds in a friendly boxing match.[19]

Soldiers returning home on leave or evacuated back to hospitals in England noticed the different civilian attitudes to their enemy; bitterness towards what was perceived as the uninformed attitudes of those back home led to many soldiers refusing to speak about their front-line experiences, unless it was with direct comrades. The popularity of old comrades' associations in the immediate post-war period was almost certainly directly influenced by this phenomenon. How could those back home really understand what life at the front was like? Shortly after the Christmas Truce, a British officer who had fraternised with the Germans on Christmas Day wrote to the *Daily Telegraph* to highlight the gap between attitudes at home and at the front:

> As I walked slowly back to the trenches I thought of Mr Asquith's sentence about not sheathing the sword until the enemy be finally crushed. It is all very well for Englishmen living at home to talk in flowing periods, but when you are out here you begin to realise that sustained hatred is impossible.[20]

When interviewed by the BBC in the 1970s, Graham Williams was asked whether his fraternisation with the enemy during the Christmas Truce led to any change in his attitude towards the Germans:

I don't think so, because even before that we thought while the truce was on it was quite all right to be friendly with them, but directly it ended well we just went back to normal. Being shot at or shooting at the other people was one of the jobs we were out there to do and we sort of took it as a matter of course. They must have regarded it in the same way. No, I don't think it made any difference, I mean even on the next day after the truce if there had been an attack or anything of the sort we'd have quite cheerfully shot them and they would have quite cheerful shot us, I'm sure of that. The people we felt most enmity towards was the German government and the German policy, the actual Germans themselves we didn't feel any hatred towards them, the individual soldiers. I mean they were out there to do their jobs just the same as we were doing ours. We didn't really hate them in any way like that, or as far as I know most of the people in our battalion didn't, I know of that. Of course there were some, I did come across people who'd had brothers or parents killed by bombs or Zeppelin raids and that sort of thing who were out to kill as many Germans as they could. But in the ordinary way we didn't feel any hatred towards them. The whole thing was absolutely in the true spirit of Christmas. The ideas of peace on earth and all the rest of it was certainly in the true spirit of Christmas. But it was only just for Christmas, I don't think it applied afterwards. It was only just during the Christmas period.[21]

The vast majority of soldiers from both sides shared this belief that the Christmas Truce was a temporary pause to the usual routine, ultimately considering themselves to be there in the trenches to get a job done. The only alternative was for the Christmas Truce and other fraternisation to have continued, leading to widespread discontent among the soldiery of both sides, resulting in mutiny and disobedience and, ultimately, an unsatisfactory end to the First World War. Instead, both sides showed themselves ready to continue when deemed necessary and were willing to use appropriate levels of aggression to this end. The casualty figures throughout the rest of the First World War reinforce this. There was a job to be done, and the soldiers on both sides were ready and professional enough to do it.

*

As the Christmas season passed and 1915 began, the multitude of factors that we have discussed in this chapter combined to ensure that ceasefires and fraternisation would still occur from time to time. But, crucially, such arrangements with the enemy would become more and more difficult to achieve, at least in an overt, organised manner. As we will see, one of the main reasons that the Christmas Truce did not recur in subsequent years was that the autonomy enjoyed by front-line fighters was gradually removed as the war developed. In 1914 it was still possible to make quick decisions at a local level which might influence a larger ceasefire or fraternisation; but in later years, the methods of fighting made this possibility increasingly unlikely. The Christmas Truce could therefore be regarded as perhaps the final moment during the First World War when individuality triumphed over the all-embracing nature of the conflict.

There would certainly be no further opportunity for a widespread truce in the same manner as the Christmas 1914 experience, in either this or any future war. Although the influence of the Christmas Truce would last for many more years to come, its real legacy lay in the fact that circumstances would combine to ensure that fraternisation was now extremely difficult to realise.

CHAPTER EIGHT

Legacy

THE CHRISTMAS TRUCE PROVED to be a crucial moment marking the end of the initial stage of the First World War. Trench fighting had now been established, the rules of this new form of conflict instituted, and the limits of individual decision-making in the front line tested to their limit. Measures would now need to be introduced by the senior command of both sides in order to prevent a repeat of the widespread fraternisation which had been witnessed at Christmas time 1914, since the incidence of ceasefires and truces were obviously counter-productive to the business of trying to win the war. As we will see, these measures were not always as successful as they were made out to be, although they certainly prevented a recurrence of the scale of the 1914 truce in future years. It might therefore be instructive to look at the immediate reactions to the event in December 1914 and how its legacy was handled at that time.

It was a common understanding among those at the front that their senior officers would forbid any attempt to establish a ceasefire or fraternisation, even for what might be considered as legitimate reasons. The surviving orders and critiques received from the generals certainly support this. Truces and fraternisation, as well as the general inertia or 'live and let live' practised in many sectors, were incompatible with the offensive spirit required to enable the execution of a war, both in terms of attack and defence. When deciding to involve himself in the Christmas Truce, Kurt Zehmisch of the 134th Infantry Regiment remained very much aware of how his German commanders would react:

Let me assure you that I for one hadn't imagined this kind of a Christmas in the trenches; but it turned out to be the most beautiful Christmas celebration I would ever experience … If this ever reaches the High Command, then woe unto us. I am confident they would be sure to relieve us of our duties, as they would fear where this could end up. We've already had word from one of the regiment's commanders who was upset and complained on account of this independent ceasefire we already have in place.[1]

On the British side, the commander who proved to be most critical was arguably General Sir Horace Smith-Dorrien, who openly condemned the whole situation once he had become aware of its full extent. Sir John French, in charge of the entire BEF, reacted in a similar way but privately may have recalled his own experience at Christmas 1900 during the Boer War, in which a short truce had been held to bury the dead. Similar criticism was expressed by Sir Douglas Haig as the newly appointed commander of First Army, whose first major order was to forbid any and all unsanctioned truces, with heavy sniping and artillery fire to recommence on 28 December in order to reinforce the point. Smith-Dorrien's subsequent routine order to Second Army on 1 January 1915 went even further in strictness, stating not only that informal understandings with the enemy were to cease but that any officers and NCOs who allowed them to take place were to be brought before a court martial.

The German reaction to the Christmas Truce was even harsher. An Army Order of 29 December served to forbid all fraternisation and communication with the enemy, specifying that any soldier choosing to contradict this order would be liable for punishment under the accusation of high treason. This order was published in both the German and Allied press, although nothing from the British side was so widely publicised or unequivocal in its intentions.

In the event, no soldier from either side appears to have faced court martial or been penalised in any significant way for involvement in the Christmas Truce, with the notable exception of officers Kenny and Welchman of the 1/39th Battalion, Garhwal Rifles. For their respective involvement in allowing their men to fraternise, both officers had their leave allowances stopped. Although one might think that this was a somewhat lenient punishment, in the circumstances it turned out to have greater implications. Both men were killed in action some months later without having had the chance to see their families for one final time. Similarly, it does not appear that any military units as a whole were punished for involvement in the truce, despite rumours circulating at the time that certain German units were relocated to the Eastern Front in order to teach them a harsh lesson.

Perhaps the higher command of both nations were influenced by the feelings of goodwill prevalent at Christmas time and decided largely to turn a blind eye to such friendliness; it would, after all, be fair to presume that it would all be forgotten once proper fighting resumed in the spring of the following year. In his memoir of 1923, Crown Prince Wilhelm reflected on the underlying feelings of benevolence inherent in the season of goodwill. He and other senior commanders would have had to have been hard-hearted indeed not to have been affected to some extent by the atmosphere of peace inherent in that particular moment.

> I will never forget the first Christmas celebration of this war. For us Germans the holy celebration of Christ is, after all, the most magnificent day of the year on which even the toughest man around displays his soft side when thinking about his childhood, his parental home and his family. That

is why I felt particularly close to my field-grey men whom I decided to join on that very day, steering my car towards the Argonnes. I spent the afternoon with the 120th and 124th Regiments in the Württembergers' camp, which consisted of clusters of huts. The fir trees of this dead forest were covered in deep snow. Shelling all around us, and the howling of bullets hissing through the air sounded angry. Otherwise the landscape was enveloped in a rather serene silence only occasionally ripped apart by gunfire intermingled by the dull detonations of mines. And yet, it was merry just about everywhere. Every trench had its own tree with candles lit and the raucous voices of men singing our beautiful old Christmas carols resonated from all sides. Kirchhoff chanted his Christmas carols on that very same evening in the trench nearest to the front where the 130th Regiment were holed up. He reported to me the following day that several Frenchmen had climbed atop the parapet and had applauded so long and so hard that he felt moved to offer an encore. In the very midst of a bitter and perfidious trench war, a miracle has happened and it was thanks to the Christmas song that a bridge had been forged between man and man.[2]

In a sense, the Christmas Truce might be regarded as an opportunity for the soldiers to 'let off steam' at an appropriate time of year, before settling back in for the hard slog that 1915 promised. In more practical terms, it was also certainly recognised that temporary ceasefires provided a useful opportunity to collect and bury the dead, while improving the condition of the front line through drainage and repair work to the trenches. Such advantages were obvious to the soldiers in the line. But what of those back home? How did they react to news of the Christmas Truce? After all, weren't each nation's troops supposed to be busy trying to win the war rather than exchanging Christmas gifts and playing football with their foes?

Letters from soldiers who had participated in the Christmas Truce or had at least witnessed the fraternisation began to arrive back home in the final days of December 1914, with quite a few notable examples seeing publication in their national and local press. Unsurprisingly, the newspapers loved such a good story, since it reflected the romantic notion of 'peace to all men' so prevalent around Christmas time and served as a suitably lighter story for readers to enjoy at that time of year instead of the usual miserable war news centring around ever-increasing casualty statistics.

The remarkable thing about press coverage of the Christmas Truce, however, was the fact that the incident was treated almost universally as an oddity quite apart from the regular war news. It was a rare example of the British press deviating from their usual portrayal of the Germans as something approaching evil baby-killing sadists. Despite recognition that in many cases the ceasefires and appeals for fraternisation were actually instigated by the Germans, the sense of kindness and humanity inherent in the event did not fit at all with the public persona of the German race and conflicted with the need to maintain constant aggression towards them. As almost a threat to the regular continuation of the war, the Christmas Truce was therefore treated as a completely separate event to the ongoing conflict. Typical of British soldiers' published reports from the front was that by Private Cecil Simnett of the 1st Battalion, North Staffordshire Regiment, printed in the *Staffordshire Sentinel* of 5 January:

> This story will be hard to swallow in England, but it is quite true. As the German trenches were not more than 50 yards away, we shouted and asked them to come over for

Christmas – just for a joke, of course; but anyway, they asked us to cease firing and sent a man out from each side between the trenches. Believe me, it was not long before we were all out, and it was arranged to cease firing until midnight Christmas. We were having cigars from them and giving them cigarettes, and singing and playing all day. Everyone else was carrying on as usual; in fact, the transport fellows came up because they could not believe it. Several of the Germans were from London and were wishing the war was over. One of them even suggested that we should finish it off at football or throwing mud at each other, as we should not get hurt. No doubt you would like to have liked to be here for the day. What funny things happen in this war![3]

As this report suggests, there was at first a certain degree of disbelief that such a thing could actually occur in the middle of a major war. The story made national front-page news in the *Daily Mirror* of 8 January 1915 as soon as photographs appeared, taken in No Man's Land by the participants and showing the fraternising troops. Any earlier doubts about the authenticity of the ceasefire were now forgotten.

While many readers of such press reports would likely have treated the Christmas Truce as an odd 'hiccup' in the course of the war, possibly considering the event an acceptable temporary break for the troops during their lives of almost constant hardship, others would point to the event with disgust since it illustrated behaviour unfitting for a loyal soldier. Patriotism was called into doubt and questions asked as to whether military orders were really being followed at the front. When such criticism of the fraternisation reached the eyes and ears of the front-line participants, it served to stoke up anger and threaten what was already a divisive relationship between those at the front and those who were not. George Ashurst, interviewed many years later, recalled this sense of annoyance at being criticised by people who had not experienced the Christmas Truce themselves or had simply misunderstood its reasoning.

> We got orders come down the trench, 'Get back in your trenches every man,' you see the armistice was finished at 1pm. By word of mouth down each trench, a fellow bobbing round out of that trench, saying to us, 'Everybody back in your trenches,' shouting. Course some of us took no damn notice. Anyway the generals behind must've seen it and got a bit suspicious so what they did, they gave orders for a battery of guns behind us to fire, and a machine gun to open out and officers to fire their revolvers at the Jerries. Of course that started the war again. Ooh we were cursing them to hell, cursing the generals and that, 'You want to get up here in this stuff never mind your giving orders, in your big chateaux and driving about in your big cars.' Yes, we hated the sight of bloody generals. We always did, all through the war ... we never liked them after that. We had papers come from England accusing us of fraternising with the Germans ... Parsons, accusing us of fraternising with the Germans! And it had been an armistice. Of course we knew it had finished at 1 o'clock, but it had been an armistice. And it was Christmas Day ... so what could you say about that? We wanted them there in front of us instead of Jerry, so we could shoot them down. Nice and safe in England, weren't they?[4]

The French and Belgian press notably chose largely to ignore the event, which seemed to be regarded as a taboo subject. The fact that such fraternisation occurred while fighting a war to defend their homeland is surely the crucial factor in understanding this attitude; French and Belgian soldiers involved in fraternisation could be seen as betraying their nation, while British involvement would be regarded as suspicious at best and perhaps treacherous at worst.

Like their British counterparts, the German press made much of the Christmas Truce, at least initially, although overall public opinion tended to be more hostile towards the participants than in Britain. Letters from German soldiers were published in the *Plauener Sonntags-Anzeiger* newspaper on 17 January 1915 under the title 'Christmas in the Field'. The soldiers themselves would usually dwell on the shared celebratory aspect of the event, portraying the Christmas Truce as an understandable pause in the war rather than part of any greater desire to prolong peace:

> You could read time and time again that the initiative had been with the Germans, which only gives testimony to the human grandeur of those serving in the army. From between the lines one could hear the longing song for peace, you couldn't miss it. 'On Christmas Eve we sang Christmas carols and played the harmonica. The English didn't shoot and they too listened ... They then called from across – we lie across from each other at a distance of 100 to 120 metres – and it wasn't before too long that the English left their trenches and walked towards us. Of course, they weren't allowed to get right inside our trenches. They felt that we should just continue making music, sing along to it as it all sounded so pretty, they said.'[5]

Kurt Zehmisch of the 134th (10th Royal Saxon) Infantry Regiment wrote home to his father, telling him the news of how he had been involved in fraternisation with the British soldiers:

> Our sergeant took three photographs of us forming a group together with the English. One often discusses the dead

comrades who had been lying in No Man's Land with no possibility in sight to bury them. The English officers felt likewise. Thus Christmas, the festival of love, meant that enemies who had been pitted against each other in hatred now, albeit briefly, became united as friends.[6]

The response from his father was rather critical of the whole thing, perhaps indicating the differing opinion of the general public back home in Germany:

> We're looking after both the English cigarettes we have received and your diary. Your encounter, or rather the encounter of all the other men – as many have written that they have met up with the English and have had conversations with them – are being criticised all around this part of the land and in part quite heavily so. If only they had been French. Just to let you know, it is above all the fanatic and war-loving politicians who are particularly and adamantly against such incidents. [These] beer politicians took special offence against German soldiers fraternising with the English whom the Kaiser had ordered by decree to be a hated entity. Rather, the only battle cry that should have been heeded was 'United we live, united we hate, we have only one enemy: England.' Taking pictures with the English … that's truly abominable. Those who own up to taking these pictures, must be severely punished. Therefore, remain vigilant. We will never know what the OHL's [Army Supreme Command] opinion is on that score, but what needs to be considered is that the main reason for this entire event was for the purpose of burying the fallen comrades.[7]

Those in Germany were, of course, somewhat detached from the reality of the front line. Just as with their counterparts in Britain, they would more often than not resort to the usual stereotypes and inaccurate characterisations promulgated by propaganda. German mother Elspeth Budde wrote to her son serving on the Polish front to tell him the news about the Christmas Truce in Flanders, which had just reached the newspapers back home. Yet rather than dwell on the humane intentions behind the event, she chose instead to emphasise the recent failed Allied attacks in that sector:

> The English thought that we, seeing we are good Christians, would set aside our weapons and wouldn't be on guard. We, of course, expected the English to play a trick on us and they certainly fell for it. The Swiss extra edition published yesterday informed us that the English suffered 3,000 dead at Nieuwpoort and had requested a truce to bury them.[8]

The danger of brotherly kinship with the enemy was used by German politicians to criticise the anti-military stance of the left and can be seen to foreshadow the allegation made after the German defeat in 1918 that the nation was 'stabbed in the back', the myth that Germany had been betrayed by trusting those who did not have the nation's global interests at heart. Although the Christmas Truce would live on in British popular memory as a heart-warming event, quite an opposite attitude would prevail in Germany. The rise of National Socialism in Germany in the 1930s would draw attention to the pacifist aspect of fraternisation in order to explain the 1918 defeat and justify calls for vengeance. A veteran of the First World War himself, Adolf Hitler was staunchly against the notion of the Christmas Truce and according to Heinrich Lugauer, one of his immediate peers during the war, allegedly made the following remark:

It should be sharply condemned that German and British soldiers join hands in No Man's Land and sing Christmas carols rather than fire at each other. Such a thing may not happen in times of war.[9]

Accurate and open historical testimony of fraternisation during the First World War became increasingly difficult to express in Germany. Such memories conflicted with the popular heroic image of the German soldier which would form the basis for the nation's official interpretation of that conflict. Under Hitler, the war was no longer portrayed as an unfortunate event which the ordinary German soldier was forced to endure, but rather something desirable and an opportunity for heroism. The Christmas Truce did not fit into this narrative at all, other than as an anomaly that might best be forgotten.

*

Keen to ensure that the Christmas Truce should be considered a redundant event and one not to be revisited, Sir John French felt the need to issue a new memorandum on 5 February 1915 which sought to remove any further temptation for fraternisation. The General Headquarters memorandum laid down new approved principles for trench warfare, stressing the importance of constant activity and encouraging aggression wherever possible. Aggression was to be the most effective form of defence, as well as being shown to improve morale. Such activity would ensure that the front-line troops had little opportunity for anything else:

> The Field-Marshal Commanding-in-Chief desires me again to draw attention to the importance of constant activity and of offensive methods in general in dealing with the enemy immediately opposed to us. For reasons known to you, we

are for the moment acting on the defensive so far as serious operations are concerned, but this should not preclude the planning and making of local attacks on a comparatively small scale, with a view to gaining ground and of taking full advantage of any tactical or numerical inferiority on the part of the enemy. Such enterprises are highly valuable, and should receive every encouragement, since they relieve monotony and improve the moral of our own troops, while they have a corresponding detrimental effect on the moral of the enemy's troops and tend in a variety of ways to their exhaustion and general disquiet.[10]

But these new directions would see only limited success, since the bad habits practised by soldiers would largely continue until methods of fighting were adapted accordingly. Other than issue regular directives, the senior commanders could do little to solve the problem of inertia since there was still too much discretion given to the infantry in the front line. At a lower level of command, many officers from both sides continued to regard ceasefires and fraternisation as useful opportunities which should be taken full advantage of. Truce arrangements provided time to collect and bury the dead without fear of being hit by shell or bullet, while also offering the chance to gather intelligence and rebuild defences. This willingness by the rank and file to embrace any possibility of a truce would inevitably result in a corresponding lack of aggression, as recognised by a German intelligence report following the outbreak of the Second Battle of Ypres in April 1915:

> Unfortunately the [French] infantry had become enfeebled by trench warfare and had lost its daring and its indifference to heavy losses and the disintegrating influence of increased enemy fire effect. The leaders and the brave-hearted fell, and

the bulk of the men, mostly inexperienced reinforcements, became helpless and only too inclined to leave the work to the artillery and trench mortars.[11]

Ultimately, it would remain very difficult for senior commanders to either identify or prove that certain individuals were involved in any fraternisation. It was often easier just to issue an informal warning and ensure that it did not happen again, as Fritz Jung found out:

> On the morning of Christmas Day, Jäger Pahl was the first one to think of walking across to the English. He shared his intention with me and we departed together. After we had returned, we found out that Captain Richter had been informed of our excursion and a severe punishment was in store for us. The commander of the battalion, however, much to our relief declined to go through with it.[12]

However, looking further ahead, trench warfare would develop in such a way to make sure that future truces and fraternisation were increasingly unlikely to occur. Physical closeness and communication with the enemy was an essential prerequisite before any significant friendships could develop, yet as artillery became more important as a weapon of war, regular bombardments served to ensure a constant flow of aggression which made ceasefires almost impossible to arrange and coordinate. The inertia experienced by infantry at the beginning of the war would be overtaken gradually by the introduction of specialised weaponry and technology which, together with a more centralised method of command, meant that trench fighters were forced into a situation of constant aggression. It was no use choosing to avoid antagonising the enemy when artillery bombardments and trench mortar units, neither under the direct control of the regular infantry battalions, were a regular feature to keep the enemy on their toes. The discretion which had been enjoyed by front-line infantry was seriously diminished and the war henceforth developed into a more controlled manner of conflict. One could argue that the war not only led to a mass loss of life, but to the death of autonomy in the case of front-line fighters. It soon became the case that it was the 'Poor Bloody Infantry' who continued to be most vulnerable to the enemy's aggression, while being the least capable of direct retaliation without orders from above. As a result, both the artillery behind the lines and mobile trench mortar units (who, introduced in 1915, tended to 'fire and retire') proved extremely unpopular among front-line troops for their habit of provoking retaliation.

Those local truces that did still manage to happen would therefore be both irregular and infrequent, and unlikely to influence other sectors. Highly visible truces were vulnerable to interference from the higher command, who would threaten to identify individuals and prosecute them. So any 'live and let live' desire would usually evolve into a more covert form of what might be called inertia: a deliberate choice of non–aggression where both antagonists shared a passive attitude. Such inertia might be due to valid reasons such as shell shortages rather than a simple desire for a peaceful existence, yet the crucial point is that this desire had to exist and be felt by both sides in order for such an arrangement to work properly. Due to the increased difficulty in arranging a proper ceasefire, the nearest thing that most units could achieve in terms of a truce would be a mixture of inertia and perfunctory aggression, the latter involving the odd instance here and there of shelling, simply because it was expected and unavoidable. This developed into a kind of ritualised form of violence, with regular shelling interspersed by moments of peace. In this way, the spirit of the Christmas Truce would live on, albeit in a much more covert manner.

*

The first real opportunity for a potential recurrence of proper fraternisation at the scale of the Christmas Truce would be the celebration of Easter in 1915. This first Easter Sunday of the war fell on 4 April, and the season of Lent was definitely marked by some German attempts to establish a ceasefire, although these were largely rebuffed by the British opposite them. As an officer of the Welch Regiment recalled:

> On Easter Day the Germans tried to fraternise showing white flags, etc. – they threw potatoes into one trench – but orders were very strict on the subject so we ignored them.[13]

Some also expected Christmas 1915 to host a rerun of the previous year's truce. But by then the war had changed considerably, taking a far nastier turn. There had been a gradual realisation on both sides that the conflict was going to be a long-running affair which would depend on a greater commitment in terms of men, munitions and all the further trappings of war. New methods of killing were introduced. Gas warfare had first been seen at the Second Battle of Ypres in April, while civilian casualties back home from enemy action were now increasingly common. The Germans began attacking English towns from Zeppelin airships in January, while their policy of unrestricted submarine warfare led to incidents such as the sinking of the passenger liner *Lusitania* in May, resulting in almost 1,200 civilian deaths. The *Lusitania* incident saw both sides receiving criticism: the Germans for showing clear aggression towards a civilian target, and the British for operating such a service in the middle of a recognised war zone. The overall result was that 1915 was characterised by a marked increase in bitterness between the two sides and by the end of the year it was difficult for anyone to feel goodwill towards their opponents. As always, the casualty statistics told the true story – by the end of the year there had been roughly 60,000 British, 140,000 German and an incredible 250,000 French casualties.

Even if a desire to fraternise had persisted in the minds of those soldiers in the front-line trenches, each nation's senior commanders ensured that there were unequivocal orders to avoid any rerun of the 1914 Christmas Truce. A confidential memorandum from the 47th (London) Division was issued on 19 December that year:

> The GOC directs me to remind you of the unauthorised truce which occurred on Christmas Day at one or two places in the line last year, and to impress upon you that nothing of the kind is to be allowed on the Divisional front this year.[14]

This instruction was reinforced by a further memo, issued at infantry brigade level:

> With reference to the above, the Brigadier wishes you to give the strictest orders to all ranks on the subject, and any man attempting to communicate either by signal or word of mouth or by any other means is to be seriously punished. All snipers and machine guns are to be in readiness to fire on any German showing above the parapet.[15]

The German authorities issued a similar directive, even harsher in tone:

Any attempt at fraternisation with the enemy (agreement not to fire, mutual visits, exchange of news, etc.) such as occurred last year at Christmas and New Year at several points on the Western Front, is strictly forbidden; this crime will be considered as verging on high treason. General HQ have issued instructions, dated the 12th inst, that fire will be opened on every man who leaves the trench and moves in the direction of the enemy without orders, as well as on every French soldier who does not make it clear that he is a deserter.[16]

It appears that in the vast majority of cases the troops obeyed their orders. Graham Williams, present when the London Rifle Brigade had been involved in the Christmas fraternisation of 1914, recalled how 1915 was indeed very different:

Actually we ourselves weren't in the trenches at Christmas, we were just out in Poperinghe, but we'd had orders just before specifically not on any account, on no account must there be any fraternising with the Germans at all. And that was quite definite and as a matter of fact we found out from a prisoner beforehand that the Germans were holding Christmas celebrations in some big barn behind the lines and our artillery got on this barn and shelled it like anything.[17]

The weather also conspired against another truce, as indicated by a letter written on Christmas Day 1915 by the German soldier Paul Diekmann, who likely served in the 55th Infantry Regiment:

I still remember Reims from last year. It was 'peace on earth', at least on Christmas Day. I myself didn't participate in the celebration in the trenches shared by some French and several of our people, as I had been dispatched to Charleville on Christmas Eve to buy gifts for the company. But I remember, the moon was shining bright and there was frost and bitterly cold. But this year – what a difference! Instead of the frost, we have rain. Instead of the festive silence, we have an artillery battle going on throughout the night. Practically without stopping. While some of our men indeed sang a few Christmas carols at about midnight on Christmas Eve, there was no response from the other side. Quite possibly that was because of the wind, as the melodies didn't carry to the English trenches. I can't and won't believe that hatred and evil would have increased to such an extent during the past gory year of the war, or that men are not able to turn towards the magical powers of Christmas Eve. God forbid![18]

However, despite circumstances conspiring against any repeat of the 1914 event, it appears that there were indeed odd, scattered examples of attempted fraternisation as well as a replication of some of the singing and other seasonal celebrations of the previous year. The most notable such incident from 1915 seems to have occurred on Christmas Day at Laventie and resulted in the court martial of two British officers. This time, the authorities were not going to sit back and accept another embarrassment like the previous year's ceasefire, and direct action was therefore needed. What transpired was later described by one of the officers, Captain Sir Iain Colquhoun of the 1st Battalion, Scots Guards:

> When having breakfast about 9am a sentry reported to me that the Germans were standing up on their parapets and walking towards our barbed wire. I ran out to our Firing Trenches and saw our men looking over the parapet and the Germans outside our barbed wire. A German officer came forward and asked me for a truce for Christmas. I replied

that this was impossible. He then asked for ¾ hour to bury his dead. I agreed. The Germans then started burying their dead and we did the same. This was finished in ½ hour's time. Our men and the Germans then talked and exchanged cigars, cigarettes, etc. for ¼ of an hour and, when the time was up, I blew a whistle and both sides returned to their trenches. For the rest of the day the Germans walked about and sat on their parapets. Our men did much the same, but remained in their trenches. Not a shot was fired.[19]

Despite the organised and short nature of the ceasefire and limited opportunity for fraternisation, those officers who sanctioned the truce were in trouble. Colquhoun and fellow Scots Guards officer Captain Miles Barne were placed under arrest and faced court martial for allowing the incident to occur. Barne was acquitted, while Colquhoun only avoided a serious reprimand thanks to his otherwise exemplary service. The military authorities clearly felt that the very public nature of the court martial, widely reported by the press, had served to make the point that such behaviour from officers would not be tolerated.

The rest of the war would see no further general desire from either side to organise a large-scale repeat of Christmas 1914. A few odd, notable exceptions can be identified, however, such as one example from Christmas Day 1916 where fraternisation occurred between Italian soldiers and the Hungarians holding the trenches opposite them:

> An object landed in our trench. We thought that it was a time-delayed bomb, but it was only a packet of cigarettes. We sent chocolate in return … Someone stuck his head above the parapet, but the snipers did not react. The faces of some Hungarians appeared. Cautiously they spoke a few hesitant words in Italian, the first that came into their head.

They just wanted to say something. The officers did not intervene; they were themselves surprised and disarmed by the unreal peaceful atmosphere in this second year of warfare in our front line trench. We outbid each other in sending presents: a little wine, dried fruit, biscuits; little things, part of our poor Christmas, of our own poverty like the poverty of the Hungarians in this rich man's war. The truce lasted till the evening.[20]

In addition, evidence certainly exists of limited truces and extended fraternisation occurring at other instances during the war. In these cases, however, such ceasefires appear to be more a direct result of the inertia and lack of aggression which came to characterise 'cushy' sectors, rather than an obvious celebration of Christmas or other holiday. However one notable exception is described in a letter written by Private Arthur Burke of the 20th Battalion, Manchester Regiment, recounting his experience of Christmas 1916 on the Western Front:

Before going any further I'll tell you how things are round here – you will hardly believe it, though you may have heard of such cases before but it's *absolutely true*. Fritz and us up here are on absolutely speaking terms – he comes over and exchanges cigs, etc. – it got so frequent it had to be stopped and even after our orders to quit two of our boys got 28 days for going out and meeting him halfway for a chat. There's never a rifle or machine-gun shot been fired by either side for many days, although we got orders to fire we knew it was hopeless to do so – so we didn't. You see both he and us are only holding shell holes which meant us going over the top for 150 yards or so and had we fired on him he would have returned the compliment so that was the understanding between us.[21]

Another much larger incident occurred on the Eastern Front in 1917 to mark Easter. Fritz Donau from Gotha recalled how his German unit began to fraternise with the Russians opposite on 15 April, the day on which Easter Sunday was celebrated in the Russian Orthodox calendar, and this arrangement continued over the following few days. Again, this event was nowhere near as widespread or long-lasting as the 1914 Christmas Truce, but remains interesting as an example of how such local ceasefires were still quite possible under the right circumstances and conditions.

> It was probably about 7am or 8am when the door of our shelter was flung open and somebody shouted: 'The Russians are coming! Get up!' Suddenly, we were wide awake, reached for our waist belts, cartridge pouches, spades and guns. But our comrade, standing guard outside told us that we wouldn't need our weapons. 'The Russians are approaching unarmed,' he said. 'They are waving to us indicating that we should come out.' We therefore climbed out of our trenches, just with our caps on and much to our surprise watched as scores of Russians emerging from their trenches, waving and gesticulating ... Very soon afterwards the German and Austrian soldiers (positioned close by) received a warm greeting from the Russians, and like brothers, were kissed on both cheeks. All animosity had disappeared. We were friends, brothers! Peace reigned on the Eastern Front.
>
> Before too long a string of lively bartering took place, food against spirits, no money changing hands. The boundless and joyful atmosphere spread through the groups accompanied by music and singing. Gesticulating, we were able to communicate with each other about the most essential things. Most importantly: peace reigned. Our officers also joined in. On the evening of 15 April 1917 little bonfires

were lit on both sides with both groups gathering together; engaging, debating with each other and celebrating. This continued into 16 April. Towards lunchtime our army band, quickly selected from the musicians from the 83rd Infantry Regiment, assembled between the two lines and offered a promenade concert lasting several hours, broken up, of course, by intermissions. Russians soldiers and ourselves promenaded or stretched out in the grass and listened. These were wonderfully balmy spring days with a sense of a peace between the two fronts such as we would never have imagined even in our dreams. Photographs were taken of little groups of Russians, Austrians and Germans. These were quickly developed and sold soon thereafter on both sides. Without any official high-level government negotiations ever having taken place, peace had been made. As we would soon find out, there was quite a bit of fraternising along the entire length of the Eastern Front all the way from the Baltic Sea down to the Carpathian Mountains. But peace didn't last long. It might have been eight or ten days that we were able to leave the war behind us and which we were lucky enough to have lived through.[22]

The notion of the temporary truce was now largely relegated to just occasional rare instances of brief ceasefires arranged to gather and bury the dead. Fraternisation was even more unusual. When communication did happen between the two sides, it was increasingly unfriendly in tone. We can point to at least one example which was far from the spirit of Christmas and much more of a simple exercise in wartime propaganda. A German unit reported that on 15 March 1915 they had discovered a box containing a newspaper and letter deposited in front of their trench. Left by the French troops opposite them, the accompanying note read as follows:

Dear German soldiers! This cruel war has been waged now for eight whole months and thousands of people are being slaughtered. Your Kaiser only uses you, in order to avail himself of honour and glory. Your wives, children and relations are dying in their own home country of famine. We have sufficient bread. Come, run across to our side, and we will look after you. Things with us are splendid, we are winning all the way.[23]

*

Later conflicts would rely on greater mobility and more advanced technology, which made the act of fighting a war an increasingly faceless experience. It had been the trench fighting that was so important to the First World War that had brought two opposing armies together for such a sustained period of time in the same location, and in so doing had encouraged friendship between foes.

The origin of subsequent conflicts also meant that the ideological reasons for fighting were often clearer to the participants, making each side more diametrically opposed to the other in a way that was not so obvious during the First World War. Knowledge of the horrors perpetrated by Nazi Germany, to give just one example, would mean that a shared chat or an exchange of souvenirs between soldiers on different sides was extremely unlikely. Harsher discipline also acted as a strong deterrent. Rather than openly declaring friendship towards their enemy, some Wehrmacht soldiers would opt for what Heinrich Böll described in his war letters as 'inner desertion', allowing him to retain his individual identity and integrity without openly questioning the war.

The idea of open, friendly fraternisation between enemies has remained in the minds of many as a uniquely First World War concept, forever linked to the Christmas Truce of 1914.

Conclusion

The Christmas Truce has enjoyed a long-lasting legacy, ultimately being depicted as a fundamental moment during the First World War. While the Somme and Ypres will always be associated with the massive casualty figures suffered by both sides as a result of the fighting in those sectors, the Christmas Truce is unique for being remembered as a moment of peace within the wider conflict. The regular re-emergence of the event as part of the traditional First World War narrative is still clearly prevalent, to the point where it has now become part of popular culture and an instantly recognisable aspect of our history. It is perhaps the special, unique nature of the Christmas Truce – the fact that such a wide-scale event did not happen again, either in the First World War or any future conflict – which makes it so memorable. The truce was the last real taste of peace before the First World War spiralled into ever-worse forms of killing. It was all downhill from there, and the nature of war would change irrevocably.

Although covered widely by the British and German press at the time, reportage of the Christmas Truce initially petered out as history moved on. The event was largely dismissed by both the published official histories and regimental records as nothing more than an amusing footnote in the larger narrative of the war, an incident of little consequence when examining the bigger picture. This is quite understandable, since the values reflected in the fraternisation which marked December 1914 simply did not fit in with the traditional ideas about fighting a war. As the conflict developed into an increasingly savage and bloody struggle, the Christmas Truce seemed increasingly at odds with it all.

Finally the question would arise as to whether the event ever really happened in the first place. Even a few months into 1915, the Christmas Truce was beginning to pass into the realms of myth. Harold Lewis, an NCO with the 240th Brigade, Royal Field Artillery, arrived on the Western Front in March 1915 and so missed experiencing the fraternisation himself. Yet despite the mass of first-hand testimony, and coloured by his own knowledge of military discipline from the later years of the war as well as the Second World War, he would express doubts as to the Christmas Truce's validity when interviewed in 1986:

> Although it would be arrogant to say that the thing didn't actually take place, I very much doubt whether anything of the nature or magnitude that has been claimed for it took place at all. People seem to imagine a level of country like Hyde Park with two lots of trenches, symmetrically facing each other and with barbed wire between them. Now the purpose of that barbed wire and the trenches, although it wasn't under ideal conditions, was to keep each side in its own place. Therefore why would anybody try to break that? And particularly because the two armies concerned, the German with that rigid discipline, and our own with the finest discipline of any fighting force there was, are not likely to break that tradition. And if anybody tried, what were the NCOs doing? What were the officers doing? I shouldn't have cared to be a young officer in a sector where that happened and have to face my CO. I think the whole thing borders on the fairy tale and may be classed with the Russians with snow on their boots and the Angels of Mons.[1]

It could be argued that the Christmas Truce made no difference whatsoever to the course of the war. It was, after all, a relatively brief moment in the larger conflict and was restricted to only certain parts of the line. By the end of the First World War, many of those soldiers involved in the Christmas Truce had been killed, with the available first-hand testimony limited to those few survivors who could recall details of that odd day or two which they spent over the Christmas season. The event would therefore become even more remote, mysterious and uncertain. It had been a break from reality, a last chance for friendship during the season of goodwill before normal service resumed. While some veterans still remembered the curious events of Christmas 1914 in Flanders very clearly, many more would only recall the usual exchange of shells or bullets. Yet its unimportance in military terms in no way meant that the truce's legacy would prove irrelevant.

Quite ordinary moments featuring proud husbands swapping photographs of their families, or young men exchanging simple Christmas gifts with one another, were transformed by the context of the battlefield to become almost magical moments which defied explanation. The romantic image of enemies shaking hands in the middle of No Man's Land, or playing football against one other, would linger on in the public consciousness to reappear at regular intervals in popular culture. The surge of interest in the history of the First World War which began in the 1960s would see the Christmas Truce feature in a broad range of books, articles and entertainments. It featured in films such as *Oh! What a Lovely War* (1969) and *Joyeux Noel* (2005); television programmes such as *Blackadder Goes Forth* ('Goodbyeee', 1989) and *Doctor Who* ('Twice Upon a Time', 2017); inspire songs from artists such as Paul McCartney ('Pipes of Peace') and The Farm ('All Together Now'); and would even be re-enacted in television adverts in order to promote the supermarket chain Sainsbury's in the centenary year of 2014. It seems that the Christmas Truce (and in particular the alleged football match, perhaps the event's most obviously visual aspect) has now become part of the short-hand symbolism used by the media when depicting the First World War. The truce is now as synonymous with that conflict as poppies, mud and war poets.

Let us leave the final word to two of the actual participants of the truce – one of them British, the other German. Private Harold Startin of the 1st Battalion, Leicestershire Regiment, was a witness to the fraternisation near Armentières on Christmas Day 1914:

> It became evident that both sides had somehow inexplicably decided to honour the season of goodwill. Everything was spontaneous and sincere. Perhaps never before, and probably never again, will the world witness such a demonstration of the 'brotherhood of man' between opposing warring forces.[2]

The diary of German officer Georg Reim offers a shorter and more succinct recollection of the fraternisation, which brings to mind the experience of so many of us at Christmas time as we enjoy the season with our family and friends and forget, just for one moment, the drudgery of ordinary life.

> [We] were happy as children at play.[3]

Acknowledgements

I WOULD PARTICULARLY LIKE to thank Eva Burke, who conducted considerable research into many of the German sources included in this book and provided fresh translations into English. Her encouragement and enthusiasm for the subject of the Christmas Truce has been greatly appreciated.

Due credit should also go to Michael Leventhal, who first came up with the idea of publishing a new history of the Truce which would feature German testimony prominently alongside British voices. As we had both worked previously with the great Malcolm Brown, we saw this project as being a very appropriate tribute in some small way to his ground-breaking work.

Peter Hart provided historical advice and encouragement which improved the book no end, for which I am immensely grateful. Many thanks also go to Jessica Cuthbert-Smith for her brilliant editing skills.

Finally, I would like to thank Natasha and Henry (and Poppy the dog) with whom I was 'locked down' over much of 2020. Much of this book was written over that long, bizarre year.

Notes

Introduction
1 The origins of this phrase are very difficult indeed to determine, and some recent investigation has suggested that in fact the quote should be more accurately used as a general indication of the feeling among many at the beginning of the First World War. While some individuals (notably Secretary for State for War Lord Kitchener and Lieutenant General Sir Douglas Haig) were openly expectant that the war would be a long-running one, it was certainly the case that families in particular hoped for a shorter affair so that their menfolk could return home by Christmas.
2 Statistics obtained from Commonwealth War Graves Commission (www.cwgc.org).
3 1st Battalion, Somerset Light Infantry, war diary (TNA, WO 95/1499/1).

1. Digging In
1 Private papers of F. L. Cassel (IWM, Documents.7405).
2 Biography included as part of the 2nd Battalion Cameronians war diary (TNA, WO 95/1715/1).
3 Interview with Henry Williamson (IWM, Sound 4257).
4 Interview with H. G. R. Williams (IWM, Sound 30545, reel 1).
5 Burgoyne, Gerald Achilles. *The Burgoyne Diaries* (London: Thomas Harmsworth Publishing Co., 1985).
6 Interview with Reginald Thomas (IWM, Sound 30, reel 4).
7 Interview with H. G. R. Williams (IWM, Sound 30545, reel 1).
8 Interview with H. G. R. Williams (IWM, Sound 30545, reel 1).
9 Interview with H. G. R. Williams (IWM, Sound 30545, reel 1).
10 Interview with H. G. R. Williams (IWM, Sound 30545, reel 1).
11 Campbell, P. J. *In the Cannon's Mouth* (London: Hamish Hamilton, 1986), pp. 218–219.

12 Interview with Albert Moren (IWM, Sound 30546, reel 1).
13 Ogle, Henry. *The Fateful Battle Line* (Barnsley: Pen & Sword, 1993), p. 42.
14 Some believe that the term originated from the Hindi word for a parasite ('chatt'), while others suggest it to be a shortened form of the medieval English word for idle gossip ('chateren').
15 Interview with Henry Williamson (IWM, Sound 4257).
16 Adams, Bernard. *Nothing of Importance: A Record of Eight Months at the Front with a Welsh Battalion* (London: Methuen & Co., 1917), p. 86.
17 Interview with H. G. R. Williams (IWM, Sound 30545, reel 1).
18 von Winterfeldt, Hans. *Meine Erlebnisse im Weltkriege, 1914–1918, Volume 1* (Württembergische Landesbibliothek, BfZ N16.4).
19 Krack, Otto. *Das deutsche Herz: Feldpostbriefe unserer Helden* (Berlin: A. Scherl, 1915).
20 Interview with Graham Greenwell (IWM, Sound 8766, reel 2).
21 Krack, Otto. *Das deutsche Herz: Feldpostbriefe unsere Helden* (Berlin: A. Scherl, 1915).
22 Krack, Otto. *Das deutsche Herz: Feldpostbriefe unsere Helden* (Berlin: A. Scherl, 1915).
23 Warneken, Bernd Jürgen. *Fraternité: Schöne Augenblicke in der Europäischen Geschichte.* (Vienna, Cologne, Weimar: Böhlau Verlag, 2016).

2. Christmas Approaches

1 Söderblom, Nathan. *Erinnern an den Ersten Weltkrieg: Materialsammlung* (Hanover: Evangelische Kirche Deutschland, 2014).
2 Open letter from the Suffragettes available at https://upload.wikimedia.org/wikipedia/commons/8/84/Open_Christmas_letter_from_the_Suffragettes_of_Manchester%2C_page_1_%2811350583266%29.jpg (accessed March 2021).
3 Private Papers of Major General Lord Loch (IWM. Documents.9350).

NOTES

4 Pope Benedict V, quoted at http://w2.vatican.va/content/bene dict-xv/it/speeches/documents/hf_ben-xv_spe_19141224_ accogliere.html (accessed March 2021.
5 12th Infantry Brigade Headquarters war diary (TNA, WO 95/1501/3).
6 12th Infantry Brigade Headquarters war diary (TNA, WO 95/1501/3).
7 Smith-Dorrien quoted by Brown, Malcolm and Seaton, Shirley. *Christmas Truce: The Western Front, December 1914* (London: Macmillan Papermac edition, 1994), pp. 35–36.
8 2nd Battalion, Essex Regiment, war diary (TNA, WO 95/1505/1).
9 Letter published by the *Aberdeen Journal* on 26 December 1914, quoted in Baker, Chris. *The Truce: The Day the War Stopped* (Stroud: Amberley Publishing, 2014).
10 Private papers of Captain R. G. Heinekey (IWM, Documents.11044).
11 Military service record of Charles Gardner Rought (TNA, WO 374/59326), quoted by Baker, Chris. *The Truce: The Day the War Stopped.*
12 Wilhelm, Crown Prince. *Meine Erinnerungen aus Deutschlands Heldenkampf* (Berlin: E. S. Mittler & Sohn, 1923).
13 Landesverein Badische Heimat e.V. and the Baden-Württemberg State Association. *Solange die Welt steht, ist soviel Blut nicht geflossen* (Baden: Rombach Verlag KG, 2014).
14 Letters featured in an article by Harald Schulze published in *Frankfurter Allgemeine Zeitung*, 24 December 2008.
15 Jürgs, Michael. *Der kleine Frieden im Grossen Krieg* (Munich: Goldmann Verlag, 2005).
16 Dehmel, Richard. *Zwischen Volk und Menschheit: Kriegstagebuch 1919* (Berlin: S. Fischer Verlag, 1919).
17 Quoted by Jürgs, Michael. *Der kleine Frieden im Grossen Krieg* (Munich: Goldmann Verlag, 2005).
18 Bernbeck, Karl. *Aus grosser Zeit: Kriegbriefe gefallener Kameraden* (Oberhess: self-published, 1936).
19 Interview with H. G. R. Williams (IWM, Sound 30545, reel 1).

20 Quoted by Jürgs, Michael. *Der kleine Frieden im Grossen Krieg* (Munich: Goldmann Verlag, 2005).
21 Letter from Karl Aldag, 18 December 1914, quoted at www.lagis-hessen.de/de/purl/resolve/subject/qhg/id/60-2 (accessed March 2021).

3. Christmas Eve in the British Sector
1 Wilhelm, Crown Prince. *Meine Erinnerungen aus Deutschlands Heldenkampf* (Berlin: E. S. Mittler & Sohn, 1923).
2 Private papers of Captain M. D. Kennedy (IWM, Documents.11097).
3 Private papers of S. Sanders (Leeds University, Liddle Collection).
4 Interview with H. G. R. Williams (IWM, Sound 30545, reel 1).
5 Lieutenant Menke, quoted by Rieker, Heinrich. *Nicht schießen, wir schießen auch nicht! Versöhnung von Kriegsgegnern im Niemandsland. 1914–1918 und 1939–1945* (Bremen: Donat, 2007).
6 Interview with Albert Moren (IWM, Sound 30546, reel 1).
7 Interview with H. G. R. Williams (IWM, Sound 30545, reel 1).
8 Interview with Albert Moren (IWM, Sound 30546, reel 1).
9 Quoted by Jürgs, Michael. *Der kleine Frieden im Grossen Krieg* (Munich: Goldmann Verlag, 2005).
10 Jung, Fritz. *Die Goslarer Jäger im Weltkrieg* (Hildesheim Buchdruckerei, August Lax: 1933).
11 Lieutenant Menke, quoted by Rieker, Heinrich. *Nicht schießen, wir schießen auch nicht! Versöhnung von Kriegsgegnern im Niemandsland. 1914–1918 und 1939–1945* (Bremen: Donat, 2007).
12 Account by 2nd Lieutenant Mervyn Richardson, attached to 2nd Battalion, Royal Welsh Fusiliers, war diary (TNA, WO 95/1365/3).
13 Letter written by 2nd Lieutenant Albert Brainerd Raynes, 27 December 1914 (University of Oxford, *First World War Poetry Digital Archive*) quoted at http://ww1lit.nsms.ox.ac.uk/ww1lit/gwa/document/9133 (accessed March 2021).
14 Interview with H. G. R. Williams (IWM, Sound 30545, reel 1).

NOTES

15 Interview with Albert Moren (IWM, Sound 30546, reel 1).
16 Quoted by Jürgs, Michael. *Der kleine Frieden im Grossen Krieg* (Munich: Goldmann Verlag, 2005).
17 Private papers of E. G. Morley (IWM, Documents.2450).
18 Private papers of H. Startin (Leeds University, Liddle Collection).
19 Jung, Fritz. *Die Goslarer Jäger im Weltkrieg* (Hildesheim: August Lax, 1933).
20 2nd Battalion, Scots Guards, war diary (TNA, WO 95/1657/3). 'F Murker' is a reference to Private Peter Murker, who would end up in German captivity after wandering too close to the enemy trenches during a subsequent occasion of fraternisation.
21 Bunnenberg, Christian. 'December 1914: Silent night in the trenches – the memory of the Christmas peace in Flanders', in Arand, Tobia (ed). *The 'Great Catastrophe' as a Reminder: History Culture of the First World War* (Münster: ZfL-Verlag, 2006).
22 Interview with H. G. R. Williams (IWM, Sound 30545, reel 1).
23 1st Battalion, Royal Irish Rifles, war diary, TNA.
24 Letter from Karl Aldag, 25 December 1914, quoted at www.lagis-hessen.de/de/purl/resolve/subject/qhg/id/60-2 (accessed March 2021).
25 Letters featured in an article by Harald Schulze published in *Frankfurter Allgemeine Zeitung*, 24 December 2008.
26 Letters featured in an article by Harald Schulze published in *Frankfurter Allgemeine Zeitung*, 24 December 2008.

4. Christmas Day in the British Sector

1 2nd Battalion, Seaforth Highlanders, war diary (TNA, WO 95/1483/1).
2 Interview with Leslie Walkinton (IWM, Sound 9132, reel 3).
3 2nd Battalion, Scots Guards, war diary (TNA, WO 95/1657/3).
4 2nd Battalion, Royal Berkshire Regiment, war diary (TNA, WO 95/1729/1).
5 Jung, Fritz. *Die Goslarer Jäger im Weltkrieg* (Hildesheim: August Lax, 1933).

6 Interview with George Ashurst (IWM, Sound 9875, reel 6).
7 Lieutenant Menke, quoted by Rieker, Heinrich. *Nicht schießen, wir schießen auch nicht! Versöhnung von Kriegsgegnern im Niemandsland. 1914–1918 und 1939–1945* (Bremen: Donat, 2007).
8 Private papers of A. Self (IWM, Documents.7753).
9 Quoted by Jürgs, Michael. *Der kleine Frieden im Grossen Krieg* (Munich: Goldmann Verlag, 2005).
10 Private papers of S. Sanders (Leeds University, Liddle Collection).
11 Interview with Henry Williamson (IWM, Sound 4257).
12 Quoted by Jürgs, Michael. *Der kleine Frieden im Grossen Krieg* (Munich: Goldmann Verlag, 2005).
13 Interview with Colin Wilson (IWM, Sound 9083).
14 Interview with Leslie Walkinton (IWM, Sound 9132, reel 3).
15 Solleder, Fridolin (ed). *Four Years on the Western Front: History of the List Regiment, 16th Reserve Infantry Regiment*, volume 76 of War Diaries of German Regiments (Munich: Schick, 1932). No such soldier can be identified, which suggests that the name was transcribed incorrectly.
16 Solleder, Fridolin (ed). *Four Years on the Western Front: History of the List Regiment, 16th Reserve Infantry Regiment*, volume 76 of War Diaries of German Regiments (Munich: Schick, 1932).
17 Interview with H. G. R. Williams (IWM, Sound 30545, reel 1).
18 Goch City Archives, Völcker-Janssen Collection, Niederrheinisches Volksblatt, Gocher Zeitung, 13.1.1915.
19 Quoted by Jürgs, Michael. *Der kleine Frieden im Grossen Krieg* (Munich: Goldmann Verlag, 2005).
20 1st Battalion, Bedfordshire Regiment, war diary (TNA, WO 95/1570/1).
21 2nd Battalion, Northamptonshire Regiment, war diary (TNA, WO 95/1722/1).
22 Quoted by Jürgs, Michael. *Der kleine Frieden im Grossen Krieg* (Munich: Goldmann Verlag, 2005).
23 2nd Battalion, Devonshire Regiment, war diary (TNA, WO 95/1712/1).

24 Sir Edward Hulse, *Letters Written From the English Front in France between September 1914 and March 1915*, privately printed in 1916 and quoted at www.archive.org/stream/letterswrittenfroohulsrich/letterswrittenfroohulsrich_djvu.txt (accessed March 2021).
25 Quoted by Jürgs, Michael. *Der kleine Frieden im Grossen Krieg* (Munich: Goldmann Verlag, 2005).
26 Interview with Ernie Williams (IWM, Sound 25228).
27 Interview with Ernie Williams (IWM, Sound 25228).
28 Quoted by Jürgs, Michael. *Der kleine Frieden im Grossen Krieg* (Munich: Goldmann Verlag, 2005).
29 Quoted by Jürgs, Michael. *Der kleine Frieden im Grossen Krieg* (Munich: Goldmann Verlag, 2005).
30 Interview with George Ashurst (IWM, Sound 9875, reel 6).
31 Interview with Walther Stennes (IWM, Sound 977, reel 1).
32 Report by Captain W. G. S. Kenny, Appendix II to the 2/39th Battalion, Garhwal Rifles war diary (TNA, WO 95/3945/3).
33 Report by Captain W. G. S. Kenny, Appendix II to the 2/39th Battalion, Garhwal Rifles war diary (TNA, WO 95/3945/3).
34 Report by Captain W. G. S. Kenny, Appendix II to the 2/39th Battalion, Garhwal Rifles war diary (TNA, WO 95/3945/3).
35 Interview with Walther Stennes (IWM, Sound 977, reel 1).
36 12th Infantry Brigade headquarters war diary (TNA, WO 95/1501/3).
37 12th Infantry Brigade headquarters war diary (TNA, WO 95/1501/3).
38 Report to 12th Infantry Brigade dated 26 December 1914 (TNA, WO 95/1501/3).
39 Interview with Leslie Walkinton (IWM, Sound 9132, reel 3).
40 Letters featured in an article by Harald Schulze published in *Frankfurter Allgemeine Zeitung*, 24 December 2008.

5. The Christmas Truce Elsewhere
1 Graves, Robert. *Goodbye to All That* (London: Jonathan Cape, 1929), p. 85.
2 Interview with Mr Rickner (IWM, Sound 4213).

3 *Bergische Arbeiterstimme*, January 1915 (Stadtarchiv Solingen).
4 Warneken, Bernd Jürgen. *Fraternité. Schöne Augenblicke in der Europäischen Geschichte.* (Vienna, Cologne, Weimar: Böhlau Verlag, 2016).
5 Stadtarchiv Viersen, Alten Gymnasium 4, 41747 Viersen, Germany.
6 Quoted by Jürgs, Michael. *Der kleine Frieden im Grossen Krieg* (Munich: Goldmann Verlag, 2005).
7 Wegener, Paul. *Flandrisches Tagebuch 1914* (Berlin: Rowohlt, 1933).
8 Rieker, Heinrich. *Nicht schießen, wir schießen auch nicht! Versöhnung von Kriegsgegnern im Niemandsland 1914–1918 und 1939–1945* (Bremen: Donat Verlag, 2007).
9 Quoted at www.traunsteiner-tagblatt.de/das-traunsteiner-tagblatt/chiemgau-blaetter/chiemgau-blaetter-2020_ausgabe,-der-erste-weltkrieg-in-feldpostbriefen-_chid,1276.html (accessed March 2021).
10 Osburg, Wolf-Rüdieger. *Hineingeworfen: Der Erste Weltkrieg in den Erinnerungen seiner Teilnehmer* (Copenhagen: Saga Egmont, 2006).
11 Albert Theodor Otto von Emmich, typescript copy of his diary (Württembergischen Landesbibliothek Stuttgart / Bibliothek für Zeitgeschichte, Bestand N60.13).
12 *Bergische Arbeiterstimme*, January 1915 (Stadtarchiv Solingen).
13 Ebeling, Fritz. *Geschichte des Infanterie-Regiments Herzog Friedrich Wilhelm von Braunschweig (Ostfriesisches) Nr. 78 im Weltkriege. Bearbeitet auf Grund der amtlichen Kriegstagebücher auf Veranlassung des Reicharchivs* (Berlin: Oldenburg i.O., 1924).
14 Rieker, Heinrich. *Nicht schießen, wir schießen auch nicht! Versöhnung von Kriegsgegnern im Niemandsland 1914–1918 und 1939–1945* (Bremen: Donat Verlag, 2007).
15 Rieker, Heinrich. *Nicht schießen, wir schießen auch nicht! Versöhnung von Kriegsgegnern im Niemandsland 1914–1918 und 1939–1945* (Bremen: Donat Verlag, 2007).
16 Boehme, Margarete. *Kriegsbriefe der Familie Wimmel* (Dresden: Carl Reissner, 1915).

17 Interview with Mr Rickner (IWM, Sound 4213).
18 Quoted by Jürgs, Michael. *Der kleine Frieden im Grossen Krieg* (Munich: Goldmann Verlag, 2005).
19 Quoted by Jürgs, Michael. *Der kleine Frieden im Grossen Krieg* (Munich: Goldmann Verlag, 2005).
20 Letter from Gotthold von Rohden, 26 December 1914, quoted at www.lagis-hessen.de/en/subjects/browse/sourceId/61/page/1/current/1/sn/qhg (accessed March 2021).
21 Letter from Gotthold von Rohden, 26 December 1914, quoted at www.lagis-hessen.de/en/subjects/browse/sourceId/61/page/1/current/1/sn/qhg (accessed March 2021).
22 Quoted at www.traunsteiner-tagblatt.de/das-traunsteiner-tagblatt/chiemgau-blaetter/chiemgau-blaetter-2020_ausgabe,-der-erste-weltkrieg-in-feldpostbriefen-_chid,1276.html (accessed March 2021).
23 Lenin quoted in Ferro, Marc et al., *Meetings in No Man's Land* (London: Constable & Robinson, 2007).

6. Boxing Day and Afterwards

1 Interview with John Wedderburn-Maxwell (IWM, Sound 9146, reel 3).
2 Interview with John Wedderburn-Maxwell (IWM, Sound 9146, reel 3).
3 Rieker, Heinrich. *Nicht schießen, wir schießen auch nicht! Versöhnung von Kriegsgegnern im Niemandsland 1914–1918 und 1939–1945* (Bremen: Donat Verlag, 2007).
4 2nd Battalion, The Queen's (Royal West Surrey Regiment), war diary (TNA, WO 95/1664/1).
5 Interview with George Ashurst (IWM, Sound 9875, reel 6).
6 von Sachsen, Prince Ernst Heinrich. *Mein Lebensweg: Vom Königsschloss zum Bauernhof* (Frankfurt: Verlag Wolfgang Weidlich, 1979).
7 20th Infantry Brigade war diary (TNA, WO 95/1650/1).
8 Letters featured in an article by Harald Schulze published in *Frankfurter Allgemeine Zeitung*, 24 December 2008.

9 Letters featured in an article by Harald Schulze published in *Frankfurter Allgemeine Zeitung*, 24 December 2008.
10 Account by an anonymous German officer (IWM, Documents.5016).
11 Interview with Colin Wilson (IWM, Sound 9083).
12 2nd Corps Summaries of Information, December 1914 (TNA, WO 157/262).
13 2nd Battalion, King's Own Scottish Borderers, war diary (TNA, WO 95/1552/2).
14 20th (Garhwal) Indian Infantry Brigade war diary (TNA, WO 95/3943/2).
15 2nd Battalion, Northamptonshire Regiment, war diary (TNA, WO 95/1722/1).
16 1st Battalion, Somerset Light Infantry, war diary (TNA, WO 95/1499/1).
17 1st Battalion, Rifle Brigade, war diary (TNA, WO 95/1496/1).
18 Interview with H. G. R. Williams (IWM, Sound 30545, reel 2).
19 Interview with H. G. R. Williams (IWM, Sound 30545, reel 1).
20 Letter from Karl Aldag, 3 January 1915, quoted at https://www.lagis-hessen.de/de/purl/resolve/subject/qhg/id/60-2 (accessed March 2021).
21 Letter from Karl Aldag, 3 January 1915, quoted at www.lagis-hessen.de/de/purl/resolve/subject/qhg/id/60-2 (accessed March 2021).
22 Dehmel, Richard. *Zwischen Volk und Menschheit: Kriegstagebuch 1919* (Berlin: S. Fischer Verlag, 1919).

7. Causes

1 Solleder, Fridolin (ed). *Four Years on the Western Front: History of the List Regiment, 16th Reserve Infantry Regiment*, volume 76 of War Diaries of German Regiments (Munich: Schick, 1932).
2 Interview with Reginald Thomas (IWM, Sound 30, reel 4).
3 Traunstein Museum of Local History, Traunstein, Germany.
4 Quoted by Jürgs, Michael. *Der kleine Frieden im Grossen Krieg* (Munich: Goldmann Verlag, 2005).
5 Interview with H. G. R. Williams (IWM, Sound 30545, reel 2).

6 von Sachsen, Prince Ernst Heinrich. *Mein Lebensweg: Vom Königsschloss zum Bauernhof* (Frankfurt: Verlag Wolfgang Weidlich, 1979).
7 Quoted by Jürgs, Michael. *Der kleine Frieden im Grossen Krieg* (Munich: Goldmann Verlag, 2005).
8 Interview with H. G. R. Williams (IWM, Sound 30545, reel 2).
9 Interview with Leslie Walkinton (IWM, Sound 9132, reel 3).
10 Quoted by Jürgs, Michael. *Der kleine Frieden im Grossen Krieg* (Munich: Goldmann Verlag, 2005).
11 Renn, Ludwig. *Krieg* (Frankfurt am Main: Frankfurter Societäts-Druckerei, 1928).
12 Quoted by Jürgs, Michael. *Der kleine Frieden im Grossen Krieg* (Munich: Goldmann Verlag, 2005).
13 Interview with Albert Moren (IWM, Sound 30546, reel 1).
14 Interview with John Wedderburn-Maxwell (IWM, Sound 9146, reel 3).
15 Ashworth, Tony. *Trench Warfare 1914–1918: The Live and Let Live System* (London: Macmillan Press, 1980), p. 211.
16 Interview with John Wedderburn-Maxwell (IWM, Sound 9146, reel 3).
17 Schober, Michael. *Zeugnisse der Unterbrechung von Gewalt im Krieg: Grundlegung einer theologischen Ethik des nicht suspendierten Zweifels* (Hildesheim: Universität Hildesheim Universitätsbibliothek, 2019).
18 Saunders, H. 'Trenches at Vimy Ridge' included in Purdom, C. B. (ed). *Everyman at War: Sixty Personal Narratives of the War* (London: JM Dent, 1939).
19 Bairnsfather, Bruce. *Bullets and Billets* (London: Grant Richards Ltd, 1916).
20 Letter from 2nd Lieutenant A. P. Sinkinson, *Daily Telegraph*, 5 January 1915.
21 Interview with H. G. R. Williams (IWM, Sound 30545, reel 2).

8. Legacy

1 Quoted by Jürgs, Michael. *Der kleine Frieden im Grossen Krieg* (Munich: Goldmann Verlag, 2005).

2 Wilhelm, Crown Prince. *Meine Erinnerungen aus Deutschlands Heldenkampf* (Berlin: E. S. Mittler & Sohn, 1923).
3 *Staffordshire Sentinel*, 5 January 1915.
4 Interview with George Ashurst (IWM, Sound 9875, reel 6).
5 *Plauener Sonntags-Anzeiger* newspaper, 17 January 1915.
6 Quoted by Jürgs, Michael. *Der kleine Frieden im Grossen Krieg* (Munich: Goldmann Verlag, 2005).
7 Quoted by Jürgs, Michael. *Der kleine Frieden im Grossen Krieg* (Munich: Goldmann Verlag, 2005).
8 Bude, Gunilla. *Feldpost für Elsbeth. Eine Familie im Ersten Weltkrieg*. (Göttingen: Wallstein Verlag, 2019).
9 Heinrich Lugauer quoted in Weber, Thomas. *Hitler's First War* (Oxford: Oxford University Press, 2010).
10 Edmonds, J. E. and Wynne, G. C. *History of the Great War: Military Operations, France and Belgium 1915*, Vol. 1, p. 33.
11 Edmonds, J. E. and Wynne, G. C. *History of the Great War: Military Operations, France and Belgium 1915*, Vol. 1, p. 213.
12 Jung, Fritz. *Die Goslarer Jäger im Weltkrieg* (Hildesheim:, August Lax, 1933).
13 Private papers of Lieutenant Colonel F. E. Packe (IWM, Documents.1653).
14 1/8th Battalion, London Regiment, war diary (TNA, WO 95/2731/2).
15 1/8th Battalion, London Regiment, war diary (TNA, WO 95/2731/2).
16 Summaries of Information, January 1915 (TNA, WO 157/4).
17 Interview with H. G. R. Williams (IWM, Sound 30545, reel 2).
18 Quoted at www.dhm.de/lemo/zeitzeugen/paul-diekmann-feldpostbriefe-aus-dem-ersten-weltkrieg-teil-i-mai-bis-dezember-1915.html (accessed March 2021).
19 Private papers of Lieutenant Colonel Sir Iain Colqhoun (IWM, Documents.6373).
20 Quoted by Olaf Mueller in Ferro, Marc et al., *Meetings in No Man's Land* (London: Constable & Robinson, 2007).
21 Private papers of A. P. Burke (IWM, Documents.1665).

22 Bechmann, Denis and Mestrup, Heinz (eds). *Wann wird das Morden ein Ende nehmen? Feldpostbriefe und Tagebucheinträge zum Ersten Weltkrieg* (Thüringen: Landeszentrale für Politische, Bildung, 2008).
23 Dirksen, Hinrich. *Käme doch bald der Friede, damit man wieder weiß, was leben heißt! Weltkriegstagebücher und Feldpost des Lehrers Dietrich Lüken aus Remels. Kriegsfreiwilliger im Infanterie Regiment Herzog Friedrich Wilhelm von Braunschweig (Ostfriesisches) Nr. 78 1914–1916* (Hinte, self-published: 2006).

Conclusion
1 Interview with Harold Lewis (IWM, Sound 9388, reel 3).
2 Private papers of H. Startin (Leeds University, Liddle Collection).
3 Quoted by Jürgs, Michael. *Der kleine Frieden im Grossen Krieg* (Munich: Goldmann Verlag, 2005).

Select Bibliography and Sources

Archives

Imperial War Museums, United Kingdom (IWM)
The National Archives, United Kingdom (TNA)

Published Works

Ashworth, Tony. *Trench Warfare 1914–1918: The Live and Let Live System* (London: Macmillan Press, 1980)
Baker, Chris. *The Truce: The Day the War Stopped* (Stroud: Amberley Publishing, 2014)
Brown, Malcolm; Seaton, Shirley. *Christmas Truce: The Western Front, December 1914* (London: Macmillan Papermac edition, 1994)
Edmonds, J. E.; Wynne, G. C. *History of the Great War: Military Operations, France and Belgium 1915* (London: Macmillan and Co., 1927)
Ferro, Marc; Brown, Malcolm; Cazals Rémy; Mueller, Olaf. *Meetings in No Man's Land: Christmas 1914 and Fraternization in the Great War* (London: Constable & Robinson, 2007)
Hart, Peter. *Fire and Movement: The British Expeditionary Force and the Campaign of 1914* (Oxford: Oxford University Press, 2015)
Jürgs, Michael. *Der kleine Frieden im Grossen Krieg* (Munich: Goldmann Verlag, 2005)
Richards, Anthony. *Wartime Christmas* (London: IWM, 2020)
Rieker, Heinrich. *Nicht schießen, wir schießen auch nicht! Versöhnung von Kriegsgegnern im Niemandsland 1914–1918 und 1939–1945* (Bremen: Donat Verlag, 2007)

SELECT BIBLIOGRAPHY AND SOURCES

Schober, Michael. *Zeugnisse der Unterbrechung von Gewalt im Krieg: Grundlegung einer theologischen Ethik des nicht suspendierten Zweifels* (Hildesheim: Universität Hildesheim Universitätsbibliothek, 2019)

Wakefield, Alan. *Christmas in the Trenches* (Stroud: Sutton Publishing, 2006)

Weintraub, Stanley. *Silent Night: The Remarkable Christmas Truce of 1914* (London: Simon & Schuster, 2001)

Index

Adams, Bernard, 26
Aisne, 42
Aisne (battle), 10–11, 24
Aldag, Karl, 57, 73–5, 158–9
'Angels of Mons', 6, 205
Anglo-Zulu War, 40
Anley, Brigadier General Frederick, 41
appeals for peace, 34–8
Argonnes, 184
Armentières, 57, 68–9, 87, 161, 207
Artois (battle), 42, 54, 118
Ashurst, George, 84, 105–6, 143, 186–7
Ashworth, Tony, 175
atrocity stories, 2, 103, 176–7
attitudes towards the enemy, 16–17, 176–9, 189–90
Auld Lang Syne (song), 99

Baden, 48
Bairnsfather, Lieutenant Bruce, 177–8
Barne, Captain Miles, 199
La Bassée, 57
Benedict XV, Pope, 36–8
Bergische Arbeiterstimme, 120–1, 128
Bernard, 2nd Lieutenant, 142
Blackadder Goes Forth (television series), 206
Boer War, 32, 40, 182
Böll, Heinrich, 203
Brandenburg, 128
British Army regiments:
  Bedfordshire Regiment, 1st Battalion, 96
  Cameronians (Scottish Rifles), 2nd Battalion, 11, 58; 5th Battalion, 98
  Cheshire Regiment, 6th Battalion, 101–3
  Devonshire Regiment, 2nd Battalion, 43, 99
  East Lancashire Regiment, 2nd Battalion, 84, 105–6
  Essex Regiment, 2nd Battalion, 41
  Gordon Highlanders, 42, 80, 87; 1/6th Battalion, 60, 87–8
  Grenadier Guards, 1st Battalion, 89–90, 148
  King's Own Scottish Borderers, 1st Battalion, 38–9; 2nd Battalion, 150–1
  Lancashire Fusiliers, 2nd Battalion, 39
  Leicestershire Regiment, 1st Battalion, 69, 151, 207
  London Regiment, 1/5th Battalion (London Rifle Brigade), 17, 24, 55–6, 60–1, 78, 93–4, 197; 13th Battalion (The Kensingtons), 151; 1/16th Battalion (Queen's Westminster Rifles), 68–9, 79–80, 115–16
  Manchester Regiment, 20th Battalion, 200
  Monmouthshire Regiment, 2nd Battalion, 98, 112–15
  Northamptonshire Regiment, 2nd Battalion, 97–8, 152
  North Staffordshire Regiment, 1st Battalion, 185–6
  The Queen's Royal Regiment, 2nd Battalion, 43
  The Queen's (Royal West Surrey Regiment), 44; 2nd Battalion, 63, 142, 174
  Rifle Brigade, 1st Battalion, 154–5; 3rd Battalion, 100
  Royal Berkshire Regiment, 2nd Battalion, 66, 82–3
  Royal Field Artillery, 45th Brigade, 19, 139–41, 163; 240th Brigade, 205

INDEX

Royal Garhwal Rifles, 2/39th Battalion, 106, 109; 1/39th Battalion, 108–9, 183
Royal Irish Rifles, 18; 1st Battalion, 72–3
Royal Scots, 42
Royal Warwickshire Regiment, 142; 1st Battalion, 177–8
Royal Welsh Fusiliers, 119; 2nd Battalion, 65–6
Scots Guards, 1st Battalion, 198–9; 2nd Battalion, 44, 71, 80–2, 87, 99–100, 160
Seaforth Highlanders, 2nd Battalion, 69, 78
Somerset Light Infantry, 1st Battalion, 4–5, 56, 153–4, 157, 169
West Yorkshire Regiment, 2nd Battalion, 86
British Army units:
  First Army, 149, 182
  Second Army, 149, 182
  II Corps, 39, 56, 149–50
  III Corps, 149
  IV Corps, 149
  Indian Corps, 43, 106, 149
  4th Division, 4–5
  7th Division, 60
  8th Division, 19, 148, 151, 163–4
  47th Division, 196
  Lahore Division, 43
  Meerut Division, 43
  11th Infantry Brigade, 17
  12th Infantry Brigade, 41, 112
  20th Infantry Brigade, 146, 151
  24th Infantry Brigade, 106
  4th Cavalry Machine Guns, 109
British Broadcasting Corporation (BBC), 178
British Expeditionary Force (BEF), 3, 10, 12, 182
Brown, Malcolm, 7
Budde, Elspeth, 190
Burgoyne, Captain Gerald, 18
burials, 43–5, 84–9
Burke, Arthur, 200

Campbell, 2nd Lieutenant Paul, 22
Cassel, F. L., 10
Le Cateau (battle), 10
Champagne (battle), 42, 54, 118
chaplains, 53, 75, 81, 86, 142
Charleville, 198
Christmas
  carol singing, 52–4, 65–9, 72–5, 77, 79, 83, 89, 135, 137, 140, 184, 188, 191, 198
  puddings, 56, 81, 139
  traditional shared elements, 46, 52
  trees, 46, 48, 5054, 57, 59, 64–5, 68–70, 74–5, 77, 87, 95, 106–7, 125–31, 134, 137, 140–2, 184
Christmas Truce
  attitude of British High Command, 182–4, 191–6, 198–9
  attitude of German High Command, 181–3, 189–93, 196–7
  Belgian involvement, 118–20, 133
  casualties during, 98–9
  causes of, 162–80 *passim*
  conclusion of, 146–8, 151–3, 160–1
  conversations with enemy during, 66, 69–70, 72, 79–82, 88–94, 96, 99–100, 105, 107–9, 113
  disbelief in, 6, 186, 205
  exchange of souvenirs during, 59, 70–1, 80–1, 89–90, 93, 99–100, 103, 107, 123, 129, 132–3, 141, 147, 158, 164, 203
  French involvement, 118–36
  legacy of, 181–207 *passim*
  public reaction to, 185–8, 204, 206–7
  trench improvements during, 83, 94, 143, 152–3, 169, 184
Cleghorn, George, 42
Colquhoun, Captain Sir Iain, 198–9
Comines, 96
Commonwealth War Graves Commission, 99
Courcy, 129
courts martial, 110–12, 170, 182–3, 198–9

Cuthbertson, Lieutenant Colonel E. B., 112–15
Cuxhaven, 55

Daily Mirror, 186
Daily Telegraph, 178
Dehmel, Richard, 51–2, 160
Dennys, 2nd Lieutenant K. G. G., 4
Deutschland über Alles (song), 52, 127
Diwali, 107
Doctor Who (television series), 206
Donau, Fritz, 201
Douve, 78

Eastern Front, 11–12
Echte, Oberjäger, 70
Easter, 195, 201–2
Ebeling, Fritz, 128–9
Edward, Prince of Wales, 148
Emmich, General Otto von, 127
Estairs, 139
exchanging souvenirs with enemy (outside Christmas), 29, 31, 39–40, 44, 168, 171, 199–200

The Farm (band), 206
Fauquissart, 82–3, 151
Festubert, 151
Fleurbaix, 87, 161
football, 5, 66, 101–2, 104–5, 186
Fournes, 57
fraternisation with enemy (before Christmas), 27–33, 38–41, 44–5
French, Field Marshal Sir John, 10, 15, 149, 182, 191
Frey, Rupert, 92, 163

Gabcke, Otto, 171
Gallipoli, 175
George V, King, 47
German Army regiments:
    7th Jäger Battalion, 83
    10th Jäger Battalion, 64
    3rd Infantry Regiment, 133
    7th Infantry Regiment, 142
    13th Infantry Regiment, 94–5
    15th Infantry Regiment, 61–2, 84–5, 87, 104–5, 124–5, 128–9, 131, 142
    16th Infantry Regiment, 49–50, 56, 91–2, 98, 106–8, 141–2, 163
    17th Infantry Regiment, 71–2, 86–7, 88–9, 96, 100
    22nd Infantry Regiment, 142
    26th Infantry Regiment, 134
    31st Infantry Regiment, 51–2
    55th Infantry Regiment, 64, 142
    68th Infantry Regiment, 122
    78th Infantry Regiment, 128–30
    83rd Infantry Regiment, 202
    104th Infantry Regiment, 113
    126th Infantry Regiment, 173
    130th Infantry Regiment, 184
    133rd Infantry Regiment, 68, 103–4
    134th Infantry Regiment, 181, 188–9
    155th Infantry Regiment, 168
    158th Infantry Regiment, 73, 171
    181st Infantry Regiment, 41
    246th Infantry Regiment, 123
German Army units:
    X Corps, 127
    XIX Corps, 41, 59–60, 143, 167
Giessen, 53
Givenchy, 43
Goch, 95
God Save the King (song), 135
Gotha, 201
Graves, Captain Robert, 119
Greenwell, Graham, 29
Gruber, Franz Xaver, 67

Hahn, Otto, 48–9, 75–6, 116, 146–7
Haig, General Sir Douglas, 149, 182
Hallesche Volksblat, 121–2
Hanbury-Tracey, Lieutenant Hon F., 81
Hartlepool, 54
Heinekey, Lieutenant Geoffrey, 43
Heinrich, Prince Ernst, 143–5, 167–8
Henderson, Major Kenneth, 109, 111
Henson, 2nd Lieutenant, 4
Herold, Max, 92
Hitler, Adolf, 190–1

INDEX

Hulse, Captain Sir Edward, 99–100
Hungarian troops, 199–200

Imperial War Museum, 7
Italian troops, 199–200

Joffre, General Joseph, 15
Joyeux Nöel (film), 206
Jung, Lieutenant Fritz, 64, 69–70, 193

Kahn, private, 131–2
Keller, Lieutenant Hans, 94–5
Kennedy, Lieutenant Malcolm, 58–9
Kenny, Captain William, 108–11, 183
Krack, Dr Otto, 29–31
Kunze, Captain, 129

Lausitz, 128
Laventie, 139, 161
Le Maisnil, 62
Lenin, Vladimir Ilyich, 138
Lepiziger Volkszeitung, 32
Leroy, Jules, 133
Le Touquet, 112
Lewis, Harold, 205
Liebesgaben (gifts), 47
Lille, 167
'live and let live' attitude, 23, 27–33, 40, 120, 131, 136, 161, 162, 169, 175, 181, 194
Lloyd, Major H. D. W., 11
Loch, Lord Douglas, 36–7
Lüdemann, Jäger, 64
Ludwig III, King, 15
Lugauer, Heinrich, 190
Lusitania, 195–6
Lys (river), 42

McCartney, Paul, 206
Magdeburg, 133
Marne (battle), 10
Mary, Princess, 47–8
Marseillaise (song), 135
Maud, Captain, 4
Meisner, Hans, 48
Menke, Lieutenant, 61, 65, 84–5

Messines, 42, 75, 101, 164
Mohr, Joseph, 67
Mons (battle), 10, 24
Moren, Albert, 23, 63, 67–8, 174
Morley, Ernest, 68–9
Mühlegg, Carl, 71–2
Murker, F., 71
Neuve Chapelle, 66, 86, 99

New Year celebrations, 155–60
Niemann, Johannes, 68, 103–4
No Man's Land, 21–3, 43–5, 64, 71, 77–161 *passim*, 166, 186, 189, 191
Nugent, Lieutenant R., 81

Oertel, Walter, 164
Ogle, Harry, 23
Oh! What a Lovely War (film), 206
Olympics of 1912, 45
orders forbidding fraternisation, 39, 41, 82, 85, 133, 148–51, 181–3, 187, 195–7
Orr, Captain, 4
Oyen, van, 122–3

Pahl, Jäger, 193
Picantin, 151
Plauener Sonntags-Anzeiger, 188
Ploegsteert, 20–1, 43, 69
Poperinghe, 197
Pravda, 138
propaganda, 16, 176, 190, 202
Prussian reputation, 29, 33, 36, 95, 109, 175, 177

'Race to the Sea', 11
Rangow, Ralf von, 129–30
Raynes, 2nd Lieutenant Albert, 66
Reagan, Jack, 100
Reim, George, 207
Reims, 124, 167, 197
religious services, 52–3, 87, 142
Renn, Ludwig, 172
Richardson, 2nd Lieutenant Mervyn, 65
Richter, Captain, 193

Rickner, german artilleryman, 119, 132–3
Riebensahm, Gustav, 104–5
Rohden, Gotthold von, 134
Romagne-sous-les-Côtes, 126
Roman Catholic Church, 36–8
Rought, 2nd Lieutenant Charles Gardner, 44–5, 142
Royal Artillery, 22
Rupprecht of Bavaria, Crown Prince, 15–16
Russian Orthodox Church, 136
Russian Revolution, 137–8
Russian Second Army, 11–12

Sainsbury's, 207
Sanders, 2nd Lieutenant Spence, 60, 87–8
Scarborough, 54
Schliepman, private, 131–2
Schober, Professor Michael, 177
Seaton, Shirley, 7
Self, Arthur, 86
Sewald, Captain Josef, 100
Stille Nacht (carol), 51, 67–9, 95, 125–7
Simnett, Cecil, 185–186
singing in the trenches, 4, 39, 46, 52–3, 66–9, 71–3, 79, 83, 89, 118, 126–27, 135, 140, 153, 157, 159, 174, 184, 186, 198, 201
Smith-Dorrien, General Sir Horace, 39–40, 149–50, 182
sniping, 22, 25–7, 38, 43, 61, 78, 86, 99, 112, 123, 127, 160, 165, 169, 182, 196, 199
Söderblom, Nathan, 34–5
Solleder, Fridolin, 91–2
Somme (battle), 23, 204
Staffordshire Sentinel, 185–6
Startin, Harold, 69, 207
Stennes, Captain Walther, 49–50, 106–8, 111–12
St Yves, 112, 177
suffragettes, 35–6

Takuli, Jemir Kushal, 109
Tannenberg (battle), 11–12
Thomas, Reginald, 19, 163–4
Thepru, Rifleman, 109
Tölke, Eduard, 64, 86–7
Traunstein, 164
trench raids, 14, 26, 112

Viersen, 122
Volz, Oberleutnant Albrecht Ludwig, 173
Vosges, 42

Walkalasika, 136–7
Walkinton, Leslie, 79–80, 90–1, 115–16, 170
Walmsley, Lieutenant, 45, 142
Warneton, 42, 49, 64
Watch on the Rhine (song), 66, 68
Wedderburn-Maxwell, 2nd Lieutenant John, 139–41, 174–6
Wegener, Paul, 124
Welch Regiment, 195
Welchman, Lieutenant, 110–11, 183
Wenzl, Josef, 141–2
Westphalia, 53
Whitby, 54
Wilhelm, Crown Prince, 46–7, 58, 183–4
Wilhelm II, Kaiser, 66
Williams, Ernie, 101–103
Williams, Graham, 16–17, 19–20, 26–7, 55–6, 60–3, 66–7, 92–4, 155–8, 166–7, 169, 178–9, 197
Williamson, Henry, 12–13, 24, 88
Wilson, Colin, 89–90, 148
Winterfeldt, General Hans von, 28
Wytschaete, 43

Ypres (First battle), 12, 13; (Second battle), 17, 192–3, 195; (Third battle), 19, 204

Zehmisch, Kurt, 181–2, 188–9
Zeppelins, 55, 179, 195